Living with Angels

Living with Angels

Guidance for your soul

Beverley Litchfield

ALLEN & UNWIN

First published in 2005

Allen & Unwin
83 Alexander Street
Crows Nest NSW 2065
Australia
Phone: (61 2) 8425 0100
Fax: (61 2) 9906 2218
Email: info@allenandunwin.com
Web: www.allenandunwin.com

National Library of Australia
Cataloguing-in-Publication entry:

Litchfield, Beverley.
Living with angels : guidance for your soul.

ISBN 1 74114 696 8.

1. Angels. 2. Future life. I. Title.

202.15

Set in 13.5/17 pt Perpetua by Bookhouse, Sydney

10 9 8 7 6 5 4 3 2 1

‘There are more things in heaven and earth, Horatio,
Than are dreamt of in your philosophy.’

Shakespeare
from *Hamlet*, Act I, Scene V

Contents

Acknowledgments

I would like to say thank you to the following people for helping this book to come to life.

I am blessed with a beautiful family and wonderful friends and I want to thank them all for their love, support and encouragement during the entire process of writing this book.

To my friend Waveney Buttle, a very special thanks for your unwavering devotion to seeing this book come to fruition.

To Annette Barlow and the team at Allen & Unwin, many thanks for your support and expertise throughout the process of getting the book published.

Finally, a special thank you to all my clients with whom I have spent many hours investigating the great world that lies beyond our own.

Foreword

It is well over twenty years now since I first met Beverley Litchfield. At that time, I was still teaching at Sydney University and, in addition to raising two teenage sons on my own, I was also attempting to work on a postgraduate thesis. Life was difficult and I was struggling. Then I heard about Beverley from some friends and, soon after, I was to experience my first ever 'reading'.

As we sat facing each other in her living room, I was dumbfounded by what she had to tell me. 'You will be a writer,' she said, unequivocally. 'You will write many books.'

Although I had enjoyed writing when I was a child, it had been many years since I had written anything. After all, it was not as though I had much free time! I simply could not imagine how this could ever come to pass and, even if it did, what would I write about? The whole idea seemed so fanciful to me at the time that I'm sure a part of me just assumed she was wrong. However, before she passed on to the next subject, I was intrigued enough to ask how she could possibly know. In her very straightforward, gentle manner, she said simply, 'I can see bookshelves filled with books—some even in other languages—and all the books have your name on their spines.' I've never forgotten that sentence. However, it was not until many years later that her prediction came true.

Over the years, while doing my research into near-death experiences, and after-death visits and angels, I have found that people are generally intrigued by stories of psychic phenomena in all their manifestations. Sceptics may dismiss this interest as suitable only for the feeble-minded, but on the contrary, I believe people are often drawn to the psychic realm as a way of honouring, understanding and corroborating their own many and varied experiences. After all, one does not have to be a gifted psychic healer such as Beverley Litchfield in order to dip into the psychic realm. Ordinary people have spontaneous extra-sensory experiences every day of the week, whether they recognise them as such or not: the person who knows who is at the other end of the phone before picking it up, the husband who talks with his deceased wife in a dream, the parent who hears the voice or feels the touch of a deceased child. However, there is a big difference between having an occasional glimpse into other realms and moving at ease within them. In order to understand and move beyond these isolated episodes, people often seek the guiding hand of a psychic.

A psychic such as Beverley is also consulted by people who want other-worldly guidance—another perspective on their life situations. Some simply want to make contact with a loved one who has passed over to the other side. Being able to give comfort to the grieving and bereaved is obviously one of her deepest pleasures, and mediumship, as you will see, is one of her greatest gifts. However, in the long history of contact with spirit forms, whether in private, or in public performances such as those of nineteenth-century stage mediums, or their more recent counterparts—the television performers who enter the living rooms of millions—what people are always intrigued by and attracted to is essentially one thing: the message that there is a life after death.

The possibility (or impossibility) of life after death occupies the mind of most of us at some point in our lives. Perhaps it takes the death of someone close to us, or, as in my own case, a near-death experience, to open us to the reality of this other world. Learning how to make sense of such experiences is of paramount importance. It is true, not all of us will be fortunate enough to have a private consultation with someone such as Beverley, but being able to 'eavesdrop' on some of these sessions by reading this wonderful book is a good starting point and a privilege indeed. As I approached the end of the book I actually slowed down my reading, I didn't want it to end. Whether you are a novice in this field or have had many years of experience working in other realms, there is so much to learn in these pages; many stories that will move you, and much simply to appreciate and enjoy.

These days, whenever I walk into my study at home I see two shelves filled with books—some in other languages—all with my name on the spines. And I smile, and think of gentle Beverley and her many gifts.

Cherie Sutherland, PhD
Author of *In the Company of Angels: Welcoming angels into your life*

Introduction

In the world we live in, we are bound by our senses. These senses are of course limited to our physical bodies. However, we are far more than just our physical senses. We have an extra sense, our insight, which gives us a link with the realm that lies beyond our own world.

Once we truly realise that we are not bound by sight and sound, and touch and taste and smell, and once we truly believe that we have insight, then we too will open the door to the realm where all truth, love and universal justice lie. In this realm there exist the souls of those who have lived on earth, but who have now travelled beyond our plane and who continue to grow and expand in this other realm.

We have also been given insight to help us deal with life's challenges. Sometimes, though, we might seek guidance outside ourselves, and this might include seeking help from those who are in touch with the realm beyond our world—psychics. These people may be able to show us an overview of our situation, as well as possible solutions to help us to see our way through the difficult patches. Certainly it is my hope that people who come to me for guidance will feel more at peace within themselves as they gain greater insight into their lives and into the life that lies beyond earthly life, although I do stress to my clients that it is important to remember that while a psychic person can be of great help we must ultimately take responsibility for solving our own problems.

It is difficult for us to comprehend how a soul can pass from our world into the next, and how they are still able to convey accurate messages to their loved ones through people with a psychic gift. While none of us fully understands how this happens, after many psychic consultations I have no doubt whatsoever that life goes on after death.

We continue to learn and grow after death, because we do not die. Of course the earthly body dies, but the spirit and soul continue on. And just as we can communicate with each other here on earth, so we can communicate with each other when we are in spirit forms. As we learn here, so we learn there.

I believe that spirits have a soul memory of their life while here on earth, and that souls do come back to earth, in order to proceed with their journey towards total enlightenment. We have many lives and many existences. As we grow, our awareness is raised and we can begin to access our wealth of truth and knowledge, which we have stored within us over many lifetimes. If we are wise while we are here on earth we will learn our lessons carefully.

I do not claim to know everything about the realm that lies beyond our current state of awareness. I merely wish to share some of my own experiences, and those of some of my clients, so that many more people might learn from this heart-warming information.

We do not need psychic gifts to access the inner wisdom that is ours. All we need is a genuine desire to seek and to use the guidance in a way that will be for our own highest good and for the good of others. If you believe in God, or a higher being, then their love will protect and guide you in your journey.

I hope also that there might be something within these pages that might assist your journey towards the light and that you will find yourself living with angels.

1

Connections with the other side

For ten years I worked as a teacher in a primary school. This was a career I enjoyed until the death of my ten day-old daughter, Katherine. This single event changed my career, my life and my entire way of thinking forever. Little did I know at that tragic time that the passing of my baby girl would end up affecting not only my own life, but the lives of many thousands of people, because it was through this catastrophic event that I became connected to the world of spirit.

Now I am able to help others to understand that life continues after we die. Many people have come to see me for assurance that their loved ones exist in spirit form, and the messages I am given assure them that all is well with those who have passed. This is possible because I have received the wonderful gift of clairvoyance and clairaudience.

My journey into the spirit world began when my beautiful daughter Katherine died. I felt as if I had been thrust into a new state of awareness. I had previously been somewhat oblivious to the realm of spirits, angels and guides, and other planes of existence. When Katherine was born my life was a busy one as I was already the mother of a beautiful son, Mark, who was then only eighteen months old. I was married to Michael, a man whom I loved dearly, and was happily living the life of housewife and mother.

Katherine was born with a birth defect known as spina bifida. She was very tiny, with lovely black hair, and as I gazed upon her for the first time my heart was brimming with love for this precious little being. The nurses called her a little angel.

I was not able to hold Katherine in my arms as she had to be taken to a major children's hospital immediately after her birth for special care. Michael and I visited her in the hospital, only to find her tiny body lost in a large humidicrib, connected to tubes and valves. I was desperately sad at the sight of my beautiful baby girl suffering as she was.

At the time, we were living in a suburb about an hour's drive from the hospital where Katherine was. I remember how excited I felt when, about a week after Katherine was born, we were told that we could bring her home from the hospital on the following day. That night I slept deeply, looking forward to having my family together and our baby at home.

At two in the morning, I suddenly awoke. I sat up in bed, feeling uneasy, with an inner sense that something was wrong. I couldn't go back to sleep so I just sat there wondering why I was feeling so strange. Twenty minutes later the telephone rang. Michael drowsily reached over to answer it, but I already knew. The worst possible news was about to be given to us. Katherine had died, her little heart could not handle the antibiotics she was given to fight off a post-operative infection. Our baby's death had occurred at 2 a.m.

This was my first encounter with the worlds beyond our own and one which opened the door to understanding. Katherine gave me this. Before she came into my life I had no knowledge of our intricate connection with the spirit world.

My early life was simple and unextraordinary. I had wonderful parents and two sisters, and we lived in a small house in the outer suburbs of Sydney. We were a very close family and Mum and Dad led by example with kindness and caring. Life was good for us. We felt loved and protected by our parents and we all thrived in this nurturing environment.

My older sister, Robyn, was my early role model. As we grew up, I admired her good looks and carefree nature. Unlike me, she was not shy and I often wished I could be as outgoing as she was. Robyn always had lots of friends and seemed so much wiser than me. It was her job to look after me, as I tagged along behind her and her friends, riding our bikes, playing tennis and attending Girl Guide meetings. I was content to be the younger sister and let Robyn look after me.

In turn I had to do the same for our youngest sister, Susan. She was a pretty little blonde girl who was clever at school and had a very sweet nature. I relished my role as mentor to Susie—it was quite a change from being a responsibility to Robyn.

The only extraordinary experience of my childhood occurred when I was about three. I remember seeing in front of me the outline of an eye—similar to the eyes drawn by ancient Egyptians in hieroglyphics. This eye followed me around, and as a toddler I thought nothing of it. I wasn't disturbed by it. I simply assumed that everyone could see eyes as well.

After I started school, the eye disappeared as I grappled with the task of fitting into a school system from which I felt alienated. I cried loudly all day every day for the first few weeks of school. I was kicked under the desk by the boy seated opposite me. He was obviously unhappy with my behaviour. From that time onwards my energies were focused on surviving the school system and then forging a pathway to a career in teaching. The psychic realm was far removed from my earthly existence.

I also remember Dad telling us that his mother had an uncanny gift of being able to predict events before they occurred. Nana had ten children, my father being the eldest. The whole family took Nana's gift for granted. One night she woke from her sleep and began to talk in a trance-like state. She told of how there would be a terrible war and that many people would die. She named the main leaders involved on both sides of the battle, including Winston Churchill (at that time almost an unknown figure) and Adolf Hitler. She also gave the names of various significant battles of the war, and then, as calmly as she had sat up, laid down and went back to sleep. The world was at peace at the time and no one believed Nana's words of warning. Her family was unphased, and quickly forgot. Time, however, proved her to be correct.

After completing high school I studied to become a school teacher. In my first year at college, I met and fell in love with Michael. He was a few years older than I and, unlike me, had survived a very difficult childhood. I felt that he had a lot to teach me about life.

Michael was born in the Ukraine and his family had suffered greatly during World War II. His parents had been separated and his father, Dimitri, was placed in a prison camp in Siberia where he was forced to work on building the Siberian railway. Anna, Michael's mother, a school teacher, was left in the village with her three young children. Times were extremely harsh and she longed for her husband. She had no idea where he had been taken, but Anna was determined to find him.

She set out in the severe Russian winter, travelling by horse and cart. It was amazing that they even survived; the family was starving and sometimes went without food for days. One night when they were resting in a barn, Anna knelt and prayed and prayed for food while the children were asleep on a pile of hay. Suddenly the room was lit by a bright light and Anna had a vision of an angel looking over her. Then, as the angel vanished before her eyes, a lamb materialised in the corner of the barn. Anna was astounded by the gift and killed and cooked the lamb to feed her starving children.

Anna finally found Dimitri, pale and ill, behind the barbed wire fence of a prison camp in Siberia. The family settled near the prison until Dimitri was released and eventually they were able to migrate to Australia.

Michael's childhood forced him to find comfort in seeking inner truths. He studied atomic physics at university, and when I first met him he was inventing electronic equipment and working in his father's business. He had many books about psychic and spiritual matters, written by Lobsang Rampa and other such authors, and I became interested in reading them too. They told of life in Tibet and the great teachers and lamas. I absorbed this knowledge, but continued on the worldly path of studying and later on marrying Michael. Before long our son, Mark, was born.

Many parents will agree that seeing your baby for the first time is a profound and spiritual experience. The sight of such a wondrous creation is both awesome and touching. When I saw Mark for the first time, I became intensely aware of a higher intelligence, a supreme creator that I refer to as God or the Supreme Being. How else could such a perfect baby be created? I still feel this every time I see a newborn baby. My family were not really religious people, but as children we went to Sunday school and church and I did believe in a higher power. Now this power had visited me and given me the gift of our son. I loved being a mother.

When my second baby, Katherine, was born, once again I felt the presence of God in creating such wonder. Even more powerful, however, were the emotions of her death. I have no doubt that Katherine's passing opened a channel within me which led me to explore the pathway towards my psychic development—the moment of her death and the feeling I experienced while she was 'visiting' me, the emotions of joy, love and sadness all at once. I now believe that if Katherine had not left this world, I would have been oblivious to the other realms of existence. After all, when we are not forced to face the loss of a dearly loved one, we have no real need to confront the issues of life and death. Through

Katherine I have been put in touch with truth at the highest level. I am grateful to her and to God for giving me this experience, and for allowing me to use my gifts of insight to help other people.

After losing Katherine, I was eager to erase the pain of her death by having another child. My prayers were answered, and a year-and-a-half later we were blessed with another beautiful baby girl. Jaynia Louise Tamara was born amidst great joy and feelings of being healed. I had been teaching at a primary school while awaiting her birth and was happy to give up my job to devote full-time care and attention to my two lovely children. I was blissfully happy. God had been truly good to me and I thrived on being a wife and mother.

As Mark and Jaynia grew up, I decided to return to my work as a primary school teacher. I really enjoyed being with the children at school. I particularly enjoyed relating to their individual personalities and I am sure that this interaction helped me to understand more about human nature. After a few years of classroom teaching, I decided to take a job as librarian in a large school. I had not been trained in library skills so this was a new challenge. By now Jaynia was nine years old and Mark had settled into high school.

Then something 'impossible' happened. Katherine sent a message to me—it was eleven years after she'd died. At that stage I knew nothing at all about life after death and I most definitely never expected that I would receive a communication from my departed baby.

It happened first thing in the morning on my first day at the new school. I was in the library when the school cleaner peeked around the corner of my office to introduce herself. As we chatted, I asked what she would be doing that day as she had already completed her morning's cleaning. To my surprise, Carmel said she would be holding a séance at her home later that day.

I had no idea what a séance was so I asked Carmel to explain. She told me that she would write out the letters of the alphabet, cut them out separately and arrange them in a circle around an overturned glass. The people attending the séance would ask questions of the spirit of the departed and the glass would then move to spell out the answers to their questions.

While this seemed quite impossible to me, I decided to ask Carmel if she would try to receive a message from my departed baby girl. I promptly forgot about our meeting and proceeded with my day.

That afternoon I was preparing to leave work when Carmel popped in and said she had something to show me. She then handed me a piece of paper which was folded over and over. As I took the paper from her, I remembered our morning conversation and eagerly unfolded it. To my utter amazement and disbelief, there before me were the words, 'Katherine Louise. I love you, Mum.'

I was dumbfounded. I could not believe my eyes and yet there it was written down in front of me. Carmel had absolutely no way of knowing that Katherine Louise was the name we had given our first baby girl. Before that morning she hadn't even met me. My understanding of life and death was altered forever by this event. I needed answers and so began my journey in the search for truth.

Just a few days after the séance, I had to purchase a large number of books for the school library. I had no idea how to go about such a task and decided to look in the local telephone directory. I skimmed through the list of 'book warehouses' and found a warehouse in a suburb a few miles away. The warehouse arranged to send a representative to the school who would then drive me to the warehouse where I could spend a few hours selecting suitable books for the library.

On the appointed day the following week an elderly man arrived at my office to escort me. Charles seemed a gentle sort of person and I felt quite at ease with him. As we drove I noticed a book in the console in front of me. It was titled 'What is Meditation?'. To make conversation I asked him about the book. Charles talked about meditation and then, surprisingly, asked me a most piercing question: 'Did I have any interest in the afterlife?'

It seemed as if I couldn't escape from this fascinating and somewhat awesome topic. I decided to tell Charles about my experience with Carmel and the message from Katherine. He nodded knowingly as I talked, and then he told me he was a spiritualist and he believed wholeheartedly in life beyond death. At the time I was amazed. It seemed like just a coincidence, yet somehow felt like more. Now I am certain that our meeting had been orchestrated from above.

At the warehouse Charles left me for a couple of hours to select my books. Even though my mind was still reeling from our conversation in the car, I enjoyed looking at the lovely new children's books and deciding which ones to order for the school library.

When Charles returned to collect me and drive me back to school, he had a stack of books in his arms which he handed to me, telling me that they would help me in my search for understanding. The books were about life beyond death and spiritualism, and I eagerly thanked him for his kindness.

Once back at school I began to feel unwell and was very relieved when the time came to go home. The next morning I was really ill. A visit to the doctor diagnosed bronchitis and I was told to stay at home to rest for the next few days. So I read my new books. I read and read, and was astounded and totally fascinated by what I was learning. I thirsted for more knowledge, and it was provided—without any preliminaries Charles posted me a book about the spiritual world each week for the next few months. He told me they were a gift from him.

As my mind struggled to process all of this information, my body struggled against illness. It seemed I just could not gather enough strength to fight off the bronchitis, and I ached from head to toe as I coughed my way through days which turned into weeks. I did not know if I would ever be well enough to return to the school, the books and children. My own children were becoming used to me being sick, and I began to feel guilty that I could not give them the attention they needed.

Then, one night, as I lay sound asleep, I was awakened by a presence beside my bed. Through dazed eyes and with utter disbelief I saw three 'beings' standing beside the bed. They were smiling peacefully at me. One held a syringe in her hand and before I could speak or take stock of the situation she pushed the needle into my neck. I felt a sharp short pain, then recovering somewhat I tried to scream. But no sound emerged. In an instant, they were gone. I thought I must have been dreaming and dozed back to sleep, but the next morning I felt so much better. My coughing had gone and I had more energy. My recovery could not be explained scientifically. I began to feel better and my health improved.

About a year later, I started to feel very tired. I visited a specialist who told me that I was suffering from an abdominal disorder which needed immediate surgical attention. There was no alternative so I was hospitalised and I underwent surgery.

Afterwards, I suffered from a post-operative infection and had a fever. As I lay asleep in the hospital bed I suddenly felt like I was flying through a tunnel. I felt an incredible sense of freedom and lightness in my body. The tunnel seemed endless and I was feeling overjoyed as I flew along. Then I flew out of the darkness of the tunnel into a brilliant white light. Within this light were three winged beings—angels. They were enormous and incredibly beautiful, radiating love and peace beyond any experience I had ever had. They pulsated with energy, which flowed through me in an energising current. I was able to see their souls which, like their bodies, also radiated love.

Then the tallest one of them, who towered above me like a skyscraper, gazed down at me and spoke. She said, 'You can come with us or you can go back to earth. It's up to you.'

I knew I had to make an immediate choice. I so much wanted to go with the angels, but I also wanted to be with my husband and children. I can't remember actually making the decision, I just said to them, 'I want to return to my children and my husband and my family on earth and I want to work.'

The angels smiled at me and the tallest one said, 'You will know this is not a dream when you wake up because of the sign of the cross on the door.'

When I woke up in the hospital room, I immediately looked for the door. Sunlight was shining through the paned window and at that moment it projected a perfect cross onto the door. The angel's words came flooding back to me, reminding me that what I had encountered was real and not a dream.

It was hard for me to understand what happened. I had already encountered the spiritual world, both through experience and my quest for knowledge, but meeting the angels at the other end of the tunnel was incredibly profound. I now know that the gifts of clairvoyance and clairaudience were given to me by the angels, but at the time I was just astounded and confused.

I went home to recover from the operation, but I found it difficult to cope. The experience of flying through the tunnel and talking to my angels had changed me. Life became very hard. How could I ever be 'normal' again? I began to long for the angels and the love and peace I had felt with them. I felt dreadful. Every day I wallowed in my misery.

After six weeks I went back to see the specialist who had performed the operation. It was clear my body was not healing properly, and so I had to keep resting and see him in another six weeks' time. Michael would get home from work and look after me. Unfortunately, all the loving support I received during this time still did not solve the problems I was facing. Nothing and no one could help me come to terms with the reality of my experience with the angels. How could life ever show me the beauty and peace which I had encountered whilst in the brilliant white light?

For many long months I languished in depression. I lost weight, and hope. I returned regularly to my doctor and after six months had passed I was finally given the 'all clear'. At last, my physical body had responded to the care and attention I was receiving, but my emotional and spiritual health continued to decline and I continued to struggle with depression.

One Sunday morning while in my usual position on the lounge, I tuned in to a religious program on television. The minister seemed a peaceful and loving man, and his inner beauty shone through. Something of my experience with the angels seemed to be evident in this man's message and, by the end of the program, a spiritual note within me had been touched at last.

This was the beginning of my recovery back to life and happiness. For the next six months I eagerly awaited the hourly program on Sunday mornings. My spiritual body soaked up the sermons and, although I was not religious, I began to feel a sense of great love for creation. More than this, my love of God gave me the strength I needed to climb slowly out of the depressed state that I had been so tightly wrapped in for twelve months. I was renewed, and my interest in life was finally restored.

I emerged from my depression with a sense of empathy for all those who suffer at mental and emotional levels. I now believe that my experience has helped me to relate to others who are suffering. I *know* how it feels to be depressed. I know how it feels to be mentally, spiritually and emotionally lost. It does not feel good, but somewhere and somehow there is always a way forward, and we will find it if we believe we can. There is always hope.

For me the way forward was the positive message I received from the Sunday sermons. But it is different for each of us. If you follow your interests, whatever they may be, you will find the way forward. For some, it may be found in study or in a hobby. For others the way forward may mean a change of life altogether—travel, career, even their home or partner.

Ask your higher self, and you will get the answer. Listen to your intuition and act on it. Most importantly, take that first step. Gradually, you will find an enthusiasm awakening in you. Your sense of powerlessness and inertia will pass, and you will find yourself charged with the joy of life.

I made a firm decision to be happy, healthy and positive about my life. No more wallowing in misery for me! Michael and I decided to move to a different suburb so that our children could benefit from a change of scenery and enjoy a better lifestyle. We found our dream house and moved in with a sense of happiness and excitement. I loved the house and enjoyed decorating it and seeing our children thriving in their new surroundings. It was a wonderful time for me and as life moved on I soon began to forget my past difficulties. I returned to my teaching position at a school where once again I was teacher-librarian. I thrived on my work and my spiritual encounters of the past seemed quite remote from the life I was now enjoying.

Alas, things took a sudden turn. As I was busy one Saturday morning cleaning my lovely home I was overcome with a sense of total exhaustion. I was physically depleted of all my energy. I lay down on the bed and felt as if the world had fallen in on top of me. Thoughts of my past ill-health came rushing in to my mind and I began to face the old fears of not being well enough to cope with my life.

I visited a local doctor to be told that I had high blood pressure and kidney stones. A surgical operation followed and the stones were removed, but I was unable to recover my energy and my spirits. I can't deny that I was languishing in depression once again.

Fortunately for me, my children were progressing with their lives. Mark and Jaynia were both doing well at school and were enjoying their pursuits in life. They had lots of friends and were both following their interests in horse riding and having fun. Michael was busy with his work and I knew that he was busy with his interests also. I was in awe of how my family were managing to keep happy and healthy while I was feeling lost and alone.

One Sunday afternoon Michael decided that we should take a drive to the Blue Mountains. He said that the fresh air would be good for me and I was too exhausted to argue, so we set out. Thankfully, my mood did change as I began to enjoy the beauty of the passing scenery. The trees were strong and nature had painted them with the most beautiful array of colours. I felt better and better. Then, to my surprise, Michael turned the car towards a little village at the foot of the mountains where some of our friends lived. Fern and Jack were a married couple whom we had known for years. In fact, Michael and Jack were friends since they first met at primary school so long ago. I met Fern when I was a guest at their wedding. She had impressed me as a most unusual and somewhat enigmatic person. She just seemed to know things and I accepted that she was somehow different from anyone else I had ever met. This fact was endorsed by what happened next.

We knocked at the door of their neat little house and were greeted with warm smiles and a genuine welcome. Soon Jack and Michael were busy chatting in the lounge room, catching up on lost time, while Fern invited me to follow her to the dining room where a table had been set for afternoon tea for the four of us. I asked how she could have done this so quickly, as we had just arrived. She smiled at me and said, 'Oh I knew you'd be coming—I told Jack this morning that you and Michael would visit this afternoon.'

I was amazed by this statement and also by her next one. 'Would you like to have a reading?' she smiled, gazing at me. Being ignorant about this subject, I enquired as to what a reading was.

'Well, I'll show you,' Fern said, taking a set of Tarot cards out of a drawer in the sideboard. Next she laid a beautiful deep-blue silk scarf on the table and proceeded to shuffle the cards. I noticed that these cards were larger than the regular playing cards, and that there were beautiful drawings on them. Fern looked at me and announced that she would now be able to tell me about myself and my life since we had last been in touch some six years earlier. She placed the cards on the silk scarf and with a great sense of purpose began to reveal to me the highs and lows of my life as if she had known every detail through first-hand experience. I was amazed and dumbfounded. She was so accurate in everything she said.

'How do you know these things?' I asked in disbelief. 'Oh it's easy,' she said. 'Being psychic is simple. It's all in there—you just have to tap into it.' This statement was the prelude to a dramatic change in my life as I tried to process the enormity of what had just transpired. I now had a quest—to discover the secrets of this incredible psychic world.

Fern telephoned me the next day and told me to pay a visit to a chiropractor whom she felt would be able to help me to get well again. I was happy to make the appointment, and upon meeting him I just knew that I would benefit from his treatments. After a few weeks I did begin to feel better and I looked forward to visiting this healer who was so significant in helping me to get well again.

A month or so later the chiropractor invited me to enter a room which had remained closed in all of my previous visits. As he ushered me into the room I was overcome with a sense of wonder as I gazed upon six amazing drawings.

'These are my spirit guides,' he proudly proclaimed. This was my first introduction to the whole concept of spirit guides. When I asked him to explain what he meant by the term 'spirit guide' he told me that I would find the answers in books. He then wrote out a list of suitable books for me to explore.

Feeling elated and somewhat eager to find the answers, I went home to begin the next part of my journey to higher awareness. My enthusiasm for life had finally returned; life began to settle down for me and I was able to continue with a greater sense of purpose.

Then, quite unexpectedly, my world changed once more. I was required to change schools. I was sent to a demonstration school to be the teacher-librarian there. I was most uncomfortable with my new role. In fact, I hated it! First, the drive to school was long and exhausting and I was pushed beyond my comfort zone. I tried to cope but it was so difficult that after only a few months I decided to resign.

I thought a lot about what to do with my life and which direction to take, and after careful consideration I decided to enroll at university to study psychology. I thought this would be a good way to learn more about the human mind. For the first three months I enjoyed the lectures, but I found myself questioning the content of the information I was studying. Somehow I felt that there was much more to the human mind than I was learning about, but at this point I was unaware of what the missing factor was. I now know that it was the spiritual aspect of human awareness that was missing. After six months I left university and I once again pondered my future.

Then, without warning, I had my first connection with the truth that angels are watching over us and assisting us with our journey through life. Unknown to me, my angels had been working hard on assisting me to higher awareness.

I was asleep in my bed when, at around 3 a.m., I was woken by an extraordinary event. Flashes of light and fire began to appear in the room. I felt dazed and astounded by what took place. Colours and fire danced before my eyes and it seemed as if the room had been hit by a tremendous fire bomb. The whole room seemed alight. Flashes appeared and faded and appeared again, and the intensity of the colours was enthralling. As I gazed on in wonder, I suddenly felt a physical sensation on my forehead. I felt as if something was lifting on my forehead right between the eyes. It felt strange and as I adjusted to the feeling of being lighter around my forehead the colours and flashes suddenly faded and disappeared, and an incredible peace settled upon me. I looked at my sleeping husband beside me. He was totally unmoved and obviously unaware of my experience. I told Michael about this event the next morning and he was interested to hear about it but, like me, was unable to explain it. Then I thought of Fern. She was obviously intended as a mentor for me on my journey to spiritual awareness and my angels nudged me to call her. She listened quietly as I told her my story and then calmly she announced, 'Your third eye has opened.'

My third eye? Whatever was that? I had no idea! Fern encouraged me to read about this phenomenon and gave me the name of a book to guide me along my way. I set off for the bookshop and I found the book quite easily. It was there on the shelf—the only copy left—so I eagerly took it and devoured all that it had to offer. I certainly agreed with what I read. It made sense—my third eye had indeed opened! I had become psychically aware.

The road to psychic awareness is a long one and there are many experiences along the way. We need to remember that we never make this journey alone. We are accompanied by our loving angels who protect us and lead us gently to our destination. So it was with me.

The next step in my journey was given to me in a dream. A week after my third eye had so dramatically opened, I dreamed of seeing a classroom. It was a kindergarten room, as evidenced by its layout. There were bare floors and plastic blocks and wooden toys. I heard a strong, loving male voice clearly say, 'You are going to become clairvoyant and you are in the kindergarten stage.' As the morning came I remembered my dream and wondered if this message was true. I had been awaiting the results of my university exams, even though I had left the course, and I looked out of the lounge room window to the letter box. Suddenly, I just knew that my results were there and that I had gained a 'c' pass. I walked to the box fully expecting the letter to be there and it was. Sure enough I had passed with a 'c'. I remembered the dream. I was clairvoyant and in kindy. But was I really? I needed more proof.

Once again my angels had been busy on the other side arranging the next step of my journey. I was shopping in the local mall with my teenage daughter and as we ambled along, enjoying our time together, Jaynia saw her friend, Heidi, coming towards us. The two girls began to chat and catch up on the last couple of years during which they had not been in touch. I was suddenly moved to say to Heidi that I knew that she had been to Fiji a month previously. She looked at me with surprise.

'How did you know?' she asked.

'I don't know,' I replied. 'I just do!'

'Well,' she said, 'you're right. I did go there and I've just returned.'

I then felt compelled to ask her about someone called Ron. She was quite taken aback and asked how I knew about Ron. Again, I don't know how I knew, I just knew! Then I remembered the dream and the prediction about me becoming clairvoyant. It must be true, I thought as we said goodbye to Jaynia's amazed friend.

At this time, I was unaware that my angels had been preparing me to use my clairvoyant gifts for a great purpose. They had obviously decided to use me to help them in their endless task of assisting people here on earth. I had my first glimpse of this a week after meeting Heidi. The phone rang one day and a woman's voice asked me if I was the Beverley about whom her friend, Heidi, had spoken. She told me her name was Jan and that she was having worries she could not handle in her life and that Heidi thought I could help her. I was not expecting this, but being of a compassionate nature I told Jan I would be happy to meet her and offer any advice I could. So it was that Jan arrived at my home later that day and somehow I tuned in to her to help guide her through her issues.

'You are amazing,' she said. 'How could you know so much about me?'

'I'm clairvoyant!' I said, feeling satisfied that I must in fact be so. After this I began to suspect that my life could be spent guiding and helping others if I so wished. However, I felt that I still needed to know more about what makes human beings how we are and who we are.

I enrolled in the College of Natural Therapies, hoping I would find more answers to my queries. I truly enjoyed the lectures and was fascinated to make discoveries about our physical selves and how best to look after ourselves. As I studied, I also became more aware psychically. Knowledge, answers and insights came flooding into my consciousness and I helped many of my fellow college students as I tuned in to their issues. Eventually, after about six months, a lecturer asked me if I would do a reading for her. I eagerly agreed and as I tuned in for her the answers came clearly and concisely, and she was delighted with the session. Then she astounded me with a question: 'Do you know that you could use this gift to diagnose illness?' Deep down within myself I knew that she was right.

So the next stage was now set in my journey to awareness and to my future work in the field of healing. At this time, I decided to enrol in the School of Hypnotic Sciences to learn about the human mind and its power. Once again, I was enthralled by the lectures, and after completing the course and passing the exams I proudly hung my Diploma of Clinical Hypnotherapy on the wall at home. I felt ready and eager to start taking clients for hypnosis and for general spiritual healings.

A fellow hypnotherapist referred a client of hers to me, not for hypnosis but for a reading. She encouraged me to charge for my services, reminding me that we all have bills to pay and that my gift deserved to be valued and rewarded. So it was that my first client, a man called John, arrived for my first professional session as a psychic. The angels were busy here, looking after me by introducing John into my life, as I soon discovered that he was a gifted spiritual healer himself, and we later worked together, giving healings to many sick people. Following that first session, John sent me a lovely bunch of flowers with a card thanking me for the wonderful help he had received via his spirit guides. I was thrilled that my first client was so happy with my work.

It wasn't long before my phone was ringing constantly as word of mouth spread and I became very busy with seeing clients. Through angelic guidance I was helping people with their personal lives as well as their health and general sense of purpose and happiness.

As I became busier, I found that keeping up with my duties as a wife and mother became more difficult and I felt I needed more freedom to continue on with my work. Something needed to change and I found myself drifting further away from my husband, even though I still loved him. Eventually, after much soul searching, I decided to move into a unit in a nearby suburb where I could see clients and have more time to myself. My children stayed at the family home with their father and were supportive of both their father and me.

Not all psychic experiences are uplifting. Some can be negative and disturbing. While I was living in my second flat in Epping, I had to deal with an experience which left me feeling defeated by the spirit world. My landlady owned two flats side by side in the same building. Not long after I'd been there she asked me to move from one to the other. It was fairly easy for my friends and me to get all my furniture and bits and pieces nicely settled into the new nest. All was well for the first month. I was busy with my clients and my family and friends.

Then one night I was awakened by a loud banging noise in the lounge room. I jumped out of bed and tiptoed in to see who or what was there. I flicked on the light switch and there was my painting of red geraniums on the floor. This explained the noise, so with relief I picked up the painting, placed it back on its hook on the wall and went back to bed.

For the next few weeks, the same thing happened every night. One by one each of the paintings, as well as a small mirror hanging in the hallway, fell off the walls. I had a couple of small paintings hanging in the bedroom. They fell off too. While I wasn't really frightened, I was starting to feel annoyed and sleep deprived.

I needed to know why this was happening so I decided to tune in to the spirit world and ask a few questions. Immediately, I saw in my mind's eye the image of an old man with grey hair and a mischievous twinkle in his eyes. He told me he didn't want me to live in his flat. It was his home, and his wife's, and they didn't want to share it. He had tried to frighten me off by making the paintings fall, but that didn't work so he decided to visit me psychically to tell me of his feelings.

After learning this information, I felt angry and upset. I didn't want to move away, but I certainly didn't want trouble either. It was obvious that the man hadn't let go of his earthly life and had not yet gone to the world beyond ours. I did not want to cause him any further trauma, but I certainly did not want him to traumatise me any more.

When my friend Sandra came to visit me a few days later, I told her about the old man. We decided that we both deserved a holiday and, as it was still winter and cold in Sydney, we chose to go north to Queensland for a touch of sunshine. After a wonderful week's holiday in the sun, I returned to my flat refreshed and more relaxed. To my disappointment, as I opened the front door, the first thing I noticed was the mirror and hall painting were on the floor. Once again my old man was up to his tricks. I had had enough! Taking action, I reached for the phone and called a real estate agent in Bondi. It was time to move. I rented a small, well-lit unit in Bondi within easy walking distance of the beach. I loved living in the busy, bustling, cosmopolitan environment of Bondi where my work kept me busy and I was happy.

Soon my work began to change somewhat and many people suffering from serious diseases such as cancer found their way to my door. I was still working with John, who had been my first client, and we focused on giving healings, comfort and support to many ill people. John had been an elder in the Mormon church and had participated in numerous hands-on healing sessions for many years. It was a blessing to have his healing gifts to offer to so many people. As the work continued on I felt fulfilled, particularly as people showed obvious benefits from consulting John and I.

Then my life changed again. It was seven years later, and I was living in a tree-lined suburb following my divorce from Michael. Mark and Jaynia were now young adults, and my life consisted of my work and enjoying special times with family and friends. It was at this point that a new man came into my life. I was introduced to Bruce through mutual friends and we were comfortable with each other from our first meeting. A year after we met we decided to marry and we moved into a lovely house in another leafy suburb. Bruce was encouraging of my work and, as a medical practitioner, he understood the intricacies of healing work.

During the first year of our marriage we travelled overseas and I enjoyed immensely learning about different lifestyles and cultures. When we returned home I continued to work and I decided to write a book about my spiritual journey thus far. *On Wings Unfolded: A journey towards the light* told of the many experiences which finally culminated in my receiving the gifts of clairvoyance and healing. While writing this book, I once more felt the presence of angels assisting me to pass on the message of their existence in our lives. So life continued on, busy and full, until once more I sensed that my world was to change.

Eventually, after thirteen years of marriage, Bruce and I decided to separate. Life is always complex and there were many factors which contributed to our decision. I am now contentedly living in an apartment which has views to the Blue Mountains, and I am still busily seeing clients and enjoying my children and grandchildren. I enjoy helping people through working with the gifts of clairvoyance and clairaudience. I 'see' pictures and I 'hear' words, which I relay back to the client. I encourage people to ask questions during their session. Angels can help us by giving information about our physical, mental, emotional and spiritual bodies. These are the areas I target during a reading.

Throughout this book, you will read more about who we are as humans, why we are never truly alone, how we can help ourselves and why we will all benefit from becoming attuned to understanding the higher states of awareness we all have access to. As you will read later on, I have had many encounters of a spiritual nature and have been privileged to see spirits and to receive messages from them to help their loved ones to a richer understanding of life here and hereafter.

If you are wondering if I am always in touch with the unseen world, then let me assure you that I am not! In general, when I am attending to the tasks of everyday living I am most unattuned to people and their spiritual sides. In fact, I really enjoy signing off psychically and shutting down my extra senses. I don't see auras while in this earthly state of awareness, and it is a real bonus for me not to receive information about people as I mingle with them in a crowd. Once, however, I broke the rule.

I was on a train, sitting near a window and watching the scenery slip by. A young woman entered the carriage and sat directly opposite me. This was at the beginning of my psychic journey and I was really testing my abilities so I decided to 'tune in'.

Immediately, I saw her life unfold before me and it made me very sad. She had two children, a boy and a girl, and they were all terribly unhappy because she was being treated badly by her unfaithful husband.

As quickly as I tuned in, I tuned out again as I realised that her life was none of my business and I was invading her privacy. I learned my lesson well and never again have I 'read' anyone in such a way. People's secrets are safe from me and I do not 'tune in' unless I'm asked to.

2

Understanding the psychic realm

The whole idea of being able to tune in to receive information is a difficult concept to comprehend. After all, it defies logic and our logical minds tell us that it is impossible to 'hear' in a manner that doesn't use our ears, to 'see' in a way that does not use our eyes, and to 'feel' our truths. Impossible? Not at all!

Within every person there is a set of extra senses. We all have been given them. Most of us have lost touch with these extra senses at a non-physical level because we are so consciously focused on surviving our everyday down-to-earth lives. To survive in our world, we need to be 'grounded', as in totally focused, on our earthly life.

There are, however, some people amongst us who are able to operate from their 'unseen' senses—we call them 'psychics', 'clairvoyants', 'mediums' or 'sensitives'. By raising their levels of conscious awareness, these people are able to receive information from their other senses.

Everyone who has these senses uses them differently. Some are clairvoyant, which means that they see pictures in a way that is rather like watching a movie in colour. Others are clairaudient, which means that they *hear* words, while others are clairsentient, which means that they *feel* the messages or truth. I receive my information from all three senses, and so I am clairvoyant, clairaudient and clairsentient.

Sometimes when I am doing a reading, it is difficult for me to capture all the information at once because I have to see, hear and feel the messages, then translate them into everyday terms. In clairvoyant messages, I see the information in pictures. Sometimes I see the pictures very clearly and sometimes not so clearly. With clairaudient messages, I see and also hear the information, which can be difficult because it often happens quickly and it is hard to keep up with the senses let alone tell the client what's happening. When I receive information through clairsentience, I simply feel that something is so. It's a knowing that is similar to the certainty with which we all know our own names.

I have often been asked how I 'tune in' to people and receive information about them. I explain that the messages I receive come from other 'spheres' or 'planes' of existence. These 'places' are vastly different from our earthly sphere.

I see them as adaptable, malleable and pliable. They seem to vibrate—radiating vast amounts of energy and peace. If you have ever been in a large cathedral or other place of worship, you have probably experienced something of this spiritual energy, which is quite overwhelming and extremely uplifting.

I believe there are many such planes of existence and as we evolve spiritually, through many lifetimes here on earth, we graduate through these planes. The first plane is where we go when we are relatively uninformed about spiritual awareness, and here we are met by spirit guides who teach us universal truths at a basic level. Through many more experiences, both on the first plane and in other incarnations on earth, we gradually evolve through the higher planes until we reach the highest—the seventh—where the soul no longer needs to incarnate back to earth and our spiritual journey is complete. We then remain with the Supreme Being because we have become perfected and therefore are united with the one who created us.

When we die our body leaves the earthly plane, but we don't journey alone. We are met by spirits and angels who take the journey with us. I have seen many souls who have been privileged enough to be carried across from this world to the next by angels. I have seen other souls who have walked or flown from this world to the next, and I have seen groups of loving spirits awaiting the new arrival of the soul on the other side.

In all cases I have seen peace and untold joy for the spirit for the new arrival and I know that after a period of adjustment the soul continues on with the wonderful journey in search for perfection of spirit.

Spirit guides from these various planes also communicate with us here on earth. It is from these spirit guides, and by using my extra senses of 'seeing', 'hearing' and 'feeling', that I receive messages and information for those who seek my help. I never filter this information, I deliver it just as I receive it.

In the same way that I receive information about other people I also receive information for my own spiritual growth. I am rarely told things about my personal life (although it does happen occasionally!) but I am often given teachings and insights about the higher realms of existence. This knowledge comes to me in different ways, but mostly clairvoyantly, in the form of visions. These visions are in colour and it is as if I'm watching a movie.

Many times I have 'travelled' to other planes, and on every plane there are halls of learning. These have the appearance of 'halls' as we understand the term in an earthly sense, but are vast, endless buildings. In my visions they are built of what appears to be white marble, with enormous columns supporting the ceilings which are of great height. Within these halls are many alcoves and rooms both small and large. These areas serve different purposes, one of which is to store universal information and all knowledge. The other purpose of these alcoves and rooms is to act as meeting places for spirit guides to greet souls who have newly arrived on the 'other side' or to teach those who are actively seeking to upgrade their awareness and spiritual knowledge.

These halls of learning parallel our own schools and universities. Just as we have students here who go to school to learn and grow, so too do spirit students in the other planes. These students are instructed by learned souls in the spirit world who are extremely evolved and who have eternal knowledge and truth which they pass on to the younger souls, allowing them to expand their consciousness.

According to Hindu and Buddhist philosophy, the halls of learning hold all knowledge. They house the akashic records, from which all truth is derived. These records house all the truths about world events and are a record of all thoughts and deeds that have taken place on earth. Souls can spend time delving into these records to learn about truth, wisdom and eternal knowledge, and at all times they have access to their spirit guides and teachers.

It is possible for those who are 'in tune' to seek these halls of learning and to tap into some of the knowledge contained within them by using their extra senses. And while it is often difficult to find the words to explain to people what I have seen or learnt, as the information I receive has no earthly equivalent, it is from these great halls of learning and the spirit guides who exist there that I receive my messages and my psychic abilities.

One of the first times I tuned in to these other planes, I had not been well and had been visiting a chiropractor for help. After a few visits I began to feel much better, and then one day he handed me his watch. 'Hold this,' he said, 'and tell me what you see and hear.'

I didn't believe I would see and hear anything, but I did as he asked. Suddenly I had a vision of an aeroplane flying over an idyllic tropical island. I saw a beautiful Asian girl and her mother. As the pictures changed I described what was happening, for about an hour. Then, when there was nothing more to be seen, I handed back the watch and asked the chiropractor if any of this made sense to him.

'You have just told me about what is happening in my life,' he said. 'The island you described is in the Philippines and the girl is my fiancée. I'm going there next month and we're going to be married. At present she lives with her mother in the Philippines. I'm going to bring her back with me to Australia after our wedding.

He then told me that he believed I had a gift, and that I would be able to help many people in the future. 'Always be true to your gift,' he said, 'and never question what you see and hear. Relay the information honestly and sincerely and your gift will never let you down.'

These words were prophetic. I went on to use psychometry, the skill of holding an object to access psychic information, and many years later I became a professional psychic. I no longer use psychometry to tune in to clients. Now I just open my psychic channel, rather like turning on a television set, and the door to their soul opens.

I like to establish a rapport with my client even if I have seen them many times previously. I like to help them to feel safe and secure with me personally and also to assure those whose first session it is that the experience will be a loving one for them. I am not open to receiving negative information and if someone is going to face a truly difficult future (such as severe illness or death of a loved one or an accident) then I am not often given this information, especially if the client cannot benefit in some way from knowing about it ahead of the event. Accidents can be avoided with the correct forewarnings so I will be given information if required on how to avoid an accident, but if I see oncoming illness or grief I will be told how the client can best deal with the issues in order to minimise the effect of it. All of my readings are delivered with love and they emanate from loving guardian angels and spirit guides and have only the best intentions for the recipient.

When the client feels at ease I ask them which areas of their life they'd like me to look at. I never seek information without permission from the client as this would be invasive and unethical. Many people like to have the session taped so I ask them to bring along an audio cassette if they wish. Once the tape is turned on I tune in and almost immediately I get a vision or hear a voice or experience a feeling concerning the issues the client is facing. Information is given at a level which best suits the client's understanding and I deliver the messages from the spirit world in a clear and concise manner.

All areas and topics can be covered and I am never phased by what I see or hear or feel. We are able to deal with topics such as relationships, health, finances, travel, emotional issues such as grief and loss of a loved one, as well as a whole range of topics relating to the practical issues of life (such as legal battles or business concerns for instance). Creative pursuits can also be dealt with and many people go on to become more creatively inspired after a psychic reading. In fact, anything one may encounter in life can be overviewed psychically.

Health readings consist of a psychic scan of the physical state of the person, discussions of particular health problems, psychic advice on diet, vitamins, minerals, herbs, and what best modalities could help, like aromatherapy, acupuncture, massage and so on. Often, a healing session will conclude with a psychic healing. This involves directing healing energy to the client, and people often remark on how warm and relaxed they feel after the session.

Many people visit psychics to settle matters of concern they are encountering in their lives at present, while others visit psychics to see what the future holds. And yet how can an event which hasn't taken place be 'seen'?

As a society, we measure time in a very practical way. We count the seconds and minutes and hours. We rely on clocks to keep us within our boundaries of time. However, I have discovered that in the real world, in the world beyond the physical world, time is of a very different nature. Time beyond our sphere is unbounded. In the physical world, time has merged into one long continuum of past, present and future, all in alignment. If we look through 'psychic eyes' at this line we can see it not as a straight line, but as a circle. This circle has no beginning and no end, and just like all circles it goes around and around.

Let me tell you of an event that took place which may help you to understand this. A dear friend of mine had asked me for a reading, and I was delighted to oblige. As I tuned in I saw a picture of my friend at a movie theatre. She was standing in the foyer with a handsome young man by her side. They were laughing and talking animatedly as they were looking at a framed poster on the wall.

As I described this scene to my friend, I told her that she would soon be visiting a movie theatre where she would be in the company of a handsome young man. When I finished describing this scene my friend turned to me, and with a surprised look on her face she told me that this scene would definitely *not* be happening in the future, because the exact scene had in fact occurred two weeks previously. Obviously I had tapped into the wheel of time at a past spot.

We do not need psychic gifts to access the inner wisdom that is ours. All we need is a genuine desire to seek and to use the guidance in a way that will be for our own highest good and for the good of others. If you believe in God, or a higher being, then their love will protect and guide you in your journey.

When we visit a psychic to find out what our future holds or for guidance in our everyday lives, it's hard to imagine how we look through the psychic's X-ray-like vision. Let me try to explain what happens. First, the psychic will be attuned to our appearance, not just our physical appearance, but also our etheric appearance—which is the appearance of a person's spiritual body, the sheath of vital forces which surround the physical body, like a kind of electrial energy force—and our name as well.

Names are really important in psychic work. Names are more than just identifiers or letters forming words, they are vibrational sounds that have very definite spiritual tones and which bring certain energies with them.

The story of Rose helps to illustrate this point. I had met Rose on a number of occasions before she made an appointment to see me. I always admired her lovely open nature and her enthusiasm for life, and I had thoroughly enjoyed our times together.

As usual, Rose arrived full of happiness, and her session revealed that all was well in her world, and that her attitude would ensure her life was bright and that any challenges she needed to face would be dealt with. We had almost reached the end of the session when Rose asked me if I would tune in and see who her spirit guide was.

A stunningly beautiful young female spirit with dark hair and black eyes emerged. Rose was told by her guide how strong and decisive she had recently become and how her guide was assisting her to find the joy and fulfilment she was seeking. The beautiful guide told Rose that it would be right to go ahead with her decision to move to a bigger house. Rose was pleased with the confirmation of her plans and felt happy with this message. Rose was told that a new man would soon appear in her life and that this man (whom Rose confirmed she had recently met by the description given) was an honest and decisive person. He would make a suitable life partner for her and she would have a happy life with him. Rose was happy with her guide's advice and thanked me for being the connection to her guide.

Then Rose asked what was the spirit's name because she wanted to seek her in meditation.

'My name is Margaret,' was the clear and definite reply.

Rose gasped with astonishment. 'I don't believe it,' she muttered. 'That's so uncanny. That's incredible!' Then Rose proceeded to tell me that Margaret was her real name—she had decided to call herself Rose because she wanted a name to suit her personality.

I was both amazed and delighted with this information. The encounter showed me the importance of names in our lives and in the spirit world, but it also demonstrated to me, once again, how wonderful it was to have our spirit guides and angels.

As we waved goodbye I reminded her, 'Don't forget Margaret,' but I doubt that Rose ever will.

Sometimes we may find ourselves attracted to a particular name. Perhaps you have always liked that particular name, even from the time you were a child. Some of us are fortunate enough to have children to whom we can give our favourite names. Others may be drawn to people with a name they like.

There may be a good spiritual reason why this occurs. A name can be so much more than simply a sound or a group of letters which, when put together, spell out a word that sounds pleasant or that conjures up positive feelings when we hear it. A name can have a spiritual source to which we are deeply connected. This was certainly the case with Denise.

Denise was about 25 years old when I met her. She was tall and healthy looking. During the session I received information which helped Denise to be more aware of her choices and to clarify her thinking. Then Denise asked about her spirit guide, and I immediately felt the presence of a female spirit. I saw a fair-haired lady named Anne who looked to be about 35 years old and was glowing with a warm clear light which radiated peace and truth.

Anne had many messages for Denise that would guide her path in life and help her spiritual growth. Anne told Denise that she was working too hard and that it would be good for her to slow down a little and to take more time to enjoy other things in her life. Denise had not been able to catch up with her friends and family for some time because she was too exhausted from her work and university studies. The guide encouraged Denise to take time to meditate as she used to do and to make sure she attended to her great love of drawing and painting.

Denise beamed when she heard these messages and said how much she had wanted to catch up with the rest of her life. Now she was determined to do so and I felt assured that her life was about to change for the better.

Denise also told me that Anne was the name she had chosen for herself at her confirmation, and it was also the name of her real mother. 'I was adopted at birth because my real mother, Anne, couldn't afford to raise me on her own,' Denise said. 'I have never met her but I always loved her anyway and the name Anne is special to me. Knowing that Anne is also my spirit guide is such a comfort and somehow makes me feel even closer spiritually to my birth mother.'

So, while our attraction to certain names may appear unimportant and random, they may in fact be connections between us and the spirit world.

Our etheric body is a force or energy which surrounds our physical body. One of the forces which permeates our physical body is our aura. This electrical field of energy surrounds all living beings, including human beings, animals and plants, appearing as a halo of light. This light can be seen radiating in various colours and intensity, depending upon the physical body it surrounds. Some of the first recordings of auras are found in religious illustrations of figures such as Jesus and Mary with haloes over their heads. These haloes are depictions of the top part of their auras.

All of us have an aura. This aura, or energy, pulsates and vibrates outside our physical body, and psychics can tell a lot about a person from the appearance and activity of their aura. I generally do not immediately see auras when I am tuning in to a client for a reading. Nor do I generally see auras when I am out in a crowd or at a gathering of people. Although I tend to psychically hear and see more readily than I read auras, I still find it a gratifying experience and much can be gleaned from auras.

Our aura is like a mirror that reflects to the outside world the inner world of us. It is in good order when we are healthy, peaceful and feeling in harmony with ourselves and our world—it shines with a brilliant white light. However, when we are distressed or not physically well, our aura will appear in darker colours and will not be radiant.

Some people have very large auras. Some have very powerful auras. I have seen, on occasion, clear, glowing auras that pulsate and project shafts of light from the person—quite an awesome sight.

In 1997, I was in Los Angeles with my second husband, Bruce, attending a conference which was organised by the Self Realization Fellowship, founded by the venerable Yogi Paramahansa Yogananda from India. It was an honour to attend the conference and learn the philosophy of this great master, but even more rewarding was an experience I had after it.

We were waiting in the hotel's underground car park for our car to be delivered to us. The car park was deserted and then I heard the chattering of gentle voices behind me. I turned to see who was coming, and was stunned by what I saw.

Walking slowly towards us was a group of nuns dressed in long saris. They made a lovely picture, moving along with their calm air of purpose. What amazed me was their auras, especially the aura of the most senior nun. Her aura extended for about three metres all around her, and it was crystal clear pure light. As she walked along, the aura pulsated, sending out sharp bursts of clear and vibrant light. I had never seen anything like it. She looked like pure light and I knew that I was in the presence of a highly evolved and enlightened soul. To this day, I have never seen such an amazing aura, and I felt fortunate that I was at the right place, at the right time, to have seen this beautiful sight.

A psychic is able to 'read' a person by tuning in to their aura. Aura reading is a valuable tool that gives us a closer understanding of who we are and which areas we could be working on to have better and healthier lives. If, for example, a psychic sees that you have a dark aura then it is your responsibility to seek the right help to heal yourself and change your aura.

The various colours of an aura can tell a psychic a lot about a person. All auras change colours according to our physical, mental, spiritual and emotional states.

A blue aura denotes a healthy physical body. If I see a royal-blue aura surrounding a person, I know that the person is well and could have been healed of an illness. Twenty-five years ago when I first went to a spiritualist church, a group of healers directed healing energy towards me and this appeared as a blue light which I absorbed. After the healing session I felt much better so I know firsthand the power of blue healing energy and I am always happy to see a person with a blue aura.

A pink aura shows that a person is undergoing a very loving stage of their life. Pink is the colour of love (spiritually speaking) and such a person is much loved, is feeling a lot of love, and is a loving being. If you feel unloved, surround yourself with pink. Wear pink clothing, decorate your environment with pink and 'think pink'. This is very powerful and can assist you to draw love into your life.

Purple is a highly spiritual colour. It is the colour used by high-ranking clergy in the church and also by royalty to denote their high status and importance, and ceremony.

When green appears in an aura, I know that, generally speaking, this person is calm and peaceful. However, if someone is jealous or envious then green may also appear in their aura.

White in an aura is amazing to behold. A white aura denotes a person of high spiritual growth, who is highly evolved and knowledgeable. Such a person is capable of giving unconditionally. A white aura is a true blessing.

If I see a person with an orange or yellow aura, I know they are either studying or going through a huge mental growth stage of their life. Orange denotes high mental activity.

I am unhappy when I see a person with a dark, dull greyish-brown or black aura. This indicates a person who is suffering from an illness or who is about to become sick. If seen in time by a psychic, such a person can be guided to prevent or overcome an illness by seeking the appropriate treatment.

A red aura displays anger and frustration. In personal relationships, if we are handling our problems well our aura will reflect this positive state by showing up peaceful colours like pink, mauve, white, pale greens and blues.

A person who is angry or resentful in their life will manifest a red aura. This is quite alarming to see. Such emotions also appear in the aura as red patches or red tones, so whenever I see red in an aura I know the person has lots of issues to resolve.

A young man with a bright red aura came to see me and I 'knew' instantly that he had a lot of unhappiness in his life. In his reading I saw how angry he was that his parents had separated when he was only five years old. He suffered from illness throughout his childhood and he lacked confidence in himself. Relationships had proven difficult for him, and he felt that he would never be happy. After his reading, in which I 'saw' a new job and a wonderful girlfriend coming into his life, he began to feel more relaxed and hopeful about his future. I noticed his aura had now changed to a lighter reddish tone and there were specks of blue and yellow on the edges, denoting less anger, and healing and more motivation for him about his life. The aura also became more 'active' as the energy within it increased. I was pleased that changes had already begun to take place, so I advised him to seek professional counselling to help deal with his anger issues and to move forward towards his future happiness.

I have also seen auras change in clients between visits to me. I have a client, Paula, who had a greyish-black aura when I first met her. As her spirit guides gave me information about her life, I understood why Paula's aura was so dark and dull. She was a lovely person who had been devastated by her life circumstances. Her husband of 30 years had recently left her and her two teenage children to find a new life with a woman he had met at work, and Paula was recovering from breast cancer.

As I 'read' her, her aura was depressing to see. She was an attractive lady who dressed well and spoke well. She had an athletic-looking body and shiny blue eyes. I could see the suffering in Paula's aura but I could also see small flecks of blue, green, pink and orange scattered throughout it so I knew she was working on her issues and that she would overcome her problems.

A couple of months after her first visit, Paula came to see me again. It was immediately apparent that her life had changed dramatically for the better. Her aura was now pink, and I saw light blues and greens within it, showing love in her life and healing and happiness. Paula had moved forwards, deciding to divorce her husband and, unexpectedly, she had met another man to whom she was attracted. Her health had improved, and she was looking forward to a happier life. By taking responsibility for herself and seeking help, Paula had changed her aura, and life, from dark and dull to shiny and bright.

The health, or ill-health, of a person is visible in their aura. If someone is sick, then the disease will manifest in the aura of that person. Illness appears first in the aura before it appears in the physical body, and various illnesses show up as different colours within the aura. Life-threatening diseases appear in very dark, dull tones, usually grey or black. I generally will not tell a person bad news about their health unless they specifically request it; however, if I see illness in an aura I will advise the client to take steps in order to prevent the illness from developing—visit a medical practitioner for a diagnosis, and then to take full responsibility for attaining good health once more. A healthy person will have a bright and clear aura, which is always a delight to see.

The aura will not only show the state of health of a person, but it will disclose the emotional state of the person as well. When someone is grieving for a loved one, or sad about how life is treating them, then this shows in the aura as brown tones, greys and dull colours. The colour of the aura will depend on how well or how poorly we are handling the situation. If we are able to place our grief or unhappiness into perspective and see the bigger picture, the aura may have dull patches of darkish colours, but also have a large amount of brighter colours within it. If we are not handling the grief or are giving in wholly to suffering, then the aura will be dull and heavy and have no trace of uplifting colours. However, as we come to terms with our unhappiness, our aura will gradually begin to change to a better state.

Fear is interesting to see in the aura, for it has ragged edges around the dull colours that present themselves. When one is fearful, the aura vibrates unevenly, and this leads to a feeling of uneasiness. Fear in an aura is easy to see psychically.

Our auras are very sensitive. When we feel uneasy in a crowded room, or when we meet someone for the first time and take an instant dislike to them, chances are that our aura has been disturbed by the crowd or particular person. We naturally gravitate towards people whose auras are compatible to our own. If there is a real difference in people's auras, then some friction may exist when these opposites meet. If someone steps inside the boundary of our aura, we might also feel uneasy and may dislike them. Auras serve as our protection in social situations. Spiritually, they also serve to protect us.

Sometimes people can temporarily house within their auras the spirits of loved ones who have passed over, although this is a rare and unusual event. A woman once came to me for a reading and the first thing I noticed was the image of a baby just above her shoulder. The baby looked to be about eighteen months old, and before we even started the reading I enquired whether the woman had lost a baby who may have been about eighteen months old. She was surprised by the question, but she had indeed lost a baby girl of that age. I then explained that I saw the baby happily snuggled into her mother's aura. The baby's spirit still needed to be with her mother, both for her own comfort until she was ready to leave our world, and to bring comfort to her mother while she adjusted to the grief of losing her daughter. I had never seen such an event before and I don't recall seeing anything like this again.

Very occasionally, a person may carry an unwanted spirit within their aura, and they will feel uneasy, sluggish, temperamental and generally de-energised. The person will not be operating at their highest potential so it is important to clear the spirit visitor away. This may be done in several ways: for example, the spirit could be acknowledged and then asked politely but firmly to leave; or a healer or psychic could perform an aura-cleansing, using powerful spiritual energy to cleanse and purify the aura, thus releasing the person of the unwelcome visitor.

We can all use our auras to protect ourselves from outside forces, so that we feel in control of our energies and achieve an inner state of balance and harmony. Here is a simple exercise for protection and light which you can use whenever you need to feel secure, calm or confident.

Each day take some time to imagine you are surrounded by white, pure light from head to toe. This light makes you feel calm and secure and protected from any negative influences. Draw an imaginary line with your hands, or just your thoughts, around yourself three times. While doing this, ask sincerely for protection and envisage yourself safe and happy, protected by the pure white light. You can then use this white light to surround you whenever you feel you need it.

We can also use our auras in meditation. Meditation is a wonderful experience, both healing and inspiring, and we can all achieve inner harmony, peace and contentment by meditating. Try the following exercise for meditating on your aura.

Start by sitting or lying comfortably in a place where you can be totally free from interruptions such as phones ringing or people entering your space. Peace and quiet is your goal. Close your eyes and allow your feelings and thoughts to surface. After a while, focus more on letting go of conscious thoughts and drifting along wherever your mind directs you. If you like, you can imagine yourself in a beautiful place such as by the ocean or a lake or in a forest, wherever you feel at one with yourself. As you drift more and more and release your cares and worries, your mind will gradually lead you into higher states of awareness and you can then begin to receive insights and knowledge beyond your usual level of consciousness.

Envisage every aspect of yourself—spiritual, emotional and physical—glowing with a pure white light, and send out love and peace and harmony to heal and balance your entire being.

This exercise will help you maintain a healthy aura; however, you will need to be very patient and be prepared to practise meditation on a regular basis, for it is only with practice that we achieve our goals of insight and awareness.

When we finally pass over, our aura, which is our life force, will go with us. Our aura is our connection with our spirit guides and other planes of existence. So it is important to keep it as pure and balanced as we can, for our wellbeing in this world, and the next.

We humans are much more complex than we might at first glance perceive ourselves to be. We have many unseen presences with us to help us through life. When we recognise why we are here on earth, we have the opportunity to grow and to develop spiritually. Our best efforts will assist us on our journey towards the next stage of our existence.

Each of us has many spirit guides and guardian angels during our lifetime. These guides come and go in harmony with our life and our growth. Sometimes spirit guides can be deceased relatives who watch over us from the other side. Sometimes they are master guides who are assigned to our souls throughout our entire existence, both here on earth as well as on other planes we will journey to between earthly incarnations. These master guides know us intimately and will be revealed to us when we pass from one lifetime to the next. They are the guides who are in charge of our being and they are directly linked to the highest being of all—the Supreme Being.

Angels are beautiful beings who should always be welcomed, without fear, and revered and honoured. They are a link of love and purity between the world in which we live and the spiritual realms. They can act as guides during our lifetimes and also for our journey to the other side.

Angels are sent to escort souls over to the other side when the time has come for them to leave this earthly plane. The angels who assist souls on their journey from this world to the next are always filled with light, love, empathy and compassion, as well as kindness and caring for the soul who has passed. They make the experience feel safe and secure for the departing soul.

I have known of people who have been introduced to the guardian angel who will take them to the other side long before their passing over actually occurs. It is my understanding that a person who is severly ill and delirious, or in a coma, or unconscious, may meet with their guardian angel while in that state. Sometimes, people have a premonition of their own death, and in that premonition they might see their angel or hear the voice of their angel telling them of their impending journey to the next world.

From the information I have gained from the many readings I have conducted over the years, I have learnt that angels usually carry children to the other side, whereas with adults they will mostly lead the way. However, I am aware that in some instances adults have been carried by angels to the other side.

Sometimes, too, the journey to the other side can be confusing if the soul is taken by surprise, as can happen with deaths by accident or sudden illness. For these souls, the angels provide a wonderful healing energy to restore any imbalance that the soul might be experiencing as a result of the illness or accident which has caused their passing over.

Some near-death experiences, however, are not so peaceful, loving and enjoyable. There are reports of people who have 'died' and returned to their bodies with accounts of the experience which range from stating they encountered absolutely nothing to experiences that sound terrifying. Why this variation occurs is not clear, but I believe the spiritual level and understanding of the person's soul has much to do with the experience they encounter. It seems that if a person is open minded, and has led a good and decent life, coming from a position of love and kindness, then they are more likely to have a positive near-death experience. However, people can be close-minded about the spiritual world and still report a positive near-death experience.

While here on earth we carry with us a blueprint of who we are at the soul level. This is our aura. This energy has life force of its own and it vibrates and pulsates to reveal the inner truths of who we are and the physical, mental, emotional and spiritual states of our being. Auras are invaluable tools to be read by psychics. Our aura is a readout of who we are and where we are going in our spiritual journey.

3

Life beyond death

In the West we are not taught that our existence can and does continue in another dimension. I believe, although I don't pretend to know how, that we do in fact continue to live beyond death. Over the many years that I have been working in the realm of psychic truth, this concept has been reinforced to me over and over again. One of the most rewarding aspects of my work is the joy that people receive when they change their feelings from grieving to relief and understanding, as they encounter messages from loved ones who have passed over to the other side.

I believe that after death the soul passes on to another plane or level of existence. I also believe that the soul will travel to a plane where it will be in harmony with the particular level of awareness that soul has reached and this will provide the best arena for further spiritual growth of that particular soul.

Like souls tend to gravitate towards each other and will find each other both here on earth as well as on other planes of existence.

Many people are curious to know about their soul mate. Who is our soul mate, and how do we know he or she is truly our soul mate or not our soul mate? There is a romantic notion that soul mates are in total love and harmony with each other. In many cases this is true. It is a wonderful notion that soul mates will meet up in this lifetime and may do so again in future lives.

Some people feel an instant inexplicable attraction for another person at first sight and can easily be led to the conclusion that they are soul mates, especially if the other party shares the attraction. Chances are that these two people have in fact found their other half, their soul mate.

What, however, is really happening here? It could be that the two people concerned must meet in this lifetime in order to complete spiritual lessons that began many years previously in other lifetimes. Nature has many ways of bringing people together; one of these is physical attraction—it is a great drawcard.

Once two people begin to explore these feelings a little further, they may begin to recognise that they have some things in common. They may both enjoy the same types of food, hobbies, work and travel destinations. They may even share the same hopes and dreams. They may then become aware of the love they have for one another and before long might even fall in love. Life sweeps them along and they feel that it's good to be alive. After an initial and sometimes extended period of getting to know each other, they could find themselves co-habitating, believing they have found in one another their true soul mate.

Then after a time, perhaps their happiness and commitment turn to dust and they each begin to feel the other person whom they loved, has let them down. They may even stop loving one another, and even begin to hate each other instead. How could they have been so wrong? Were they blinded by their love, or deceived by the gods? Did their spirit guides lead them down a dead-end? Or are they just foolish?

They could well become disillusioned at this point; indeed, many do. At this stage they might well turn away from their beliefs in life and goodness and happiness, as they become confused, despairing and lost.

As a clairvoyant counsellor, I have seen many people at this stage of despair. This is when we all begin to question the whole concept of truth bringing us happiness, and often we can become rocked to our very foundations. How could our soul mate cause us such angst and unhappiness?

Well, the truth is that our soul mate is not only in our life to bring us joy and perfect harmony and peace. Our true soul mate must also bring us the lessons that we need to encounter in order for us to grow.

True soul mates meet each other in many lifetimes and are each other's master teachers. They will share joy and disasters together. They may or may not be together in a life situation in a particular earthly existence. We may need to meet our soul mate only to be separated by death or incompatibility. To be complete, a relationship must contain all of the emotions that a person has the capacity to experience—including love and hatred, anger, frustration, sadness and joy, peace and confusion.

Whatever the situation between them, if they are soul mates, they will have agreed to whatever life unveils for them before they enter their earthly bodies. They may or may not agree to meet each other on the next plane after they pass into the world beyond this. They may decide that one will be the spirit guide for the other when one soul mate passes over before the other. They may choose to incarnate together in the next earthly life and will definitely have chosen to complete the lessons they mutually have, whether it takes one lifetime or more.

Our soul mate is someone we know inside out. Soul mates will be together forever—sometimes loving, sometimes hating, sometimes happily, sometimes sadly, but *always* with the knowledge that something very powerful is drawing their souls so closely together that their souls are true mates for each other, just as the two of them are. If you feel you have found your soul mate, be open to all of life's experiences with them and be prepared to love them and/or let them go if the situation requires this. You will definitely meet again, until your two souls are so much in harmony with each other that they merge and become truly one.

When two souls merge, they are joined together like two peas in a pod. They remain separate beings, but they share an unbreakable common bond which holds them together forever. They retain their own individual characteristics and souls, but are each a part of the whole soul, which they share equally. The two beings do not merge to become one person—they are still two separate people who have their souls merged or share the oneness of all things. This then is the true meaning of soul mates.

The story of Emily is one which illustrates this well. Emily came for a reading when she was dealing with the difficulties of divorcing Joshua, her husband of twenty years. They had tried to make the marriage work, but after a trial separation they decided to divorce. Emily was frightened of a life without Joshua, but realised there were too many problems between them and accepted that she should move on for her own sake and that of her children.

As I tuned in to her I saw that she would soon spend a few weeks on holiday with her two daughters. She agreed that she planned to visit the north coast and have a holiday by the ocean. I saw in the reading that she would meet a man who would pay her a lot of attention. She left her session feeling positive and determined to get through her problems with the divorce and enjoy her forthcoming holiday.

Six months after her first reading Emily came to see me again. She excitedly told me that the man I had seen in her meeting did in fact appear in her life. To her amazement she accidentally bumped into an old friend whom she had not seen since she was in her twenties. She had gone out with Edward for about six months but then he took a job in the country and they lost touch. She had been lying by the pool when Edward saw her. He asked her if her name was Emily and she immediately recognised him. With joy, all the feelings she had for him flooded back to her and she found herself calling out his name. They could not stop themselves from hugging each other.

She was delighted to tell me that he too was divorced and that they had decided to spend more time getting to know each other again, and now that they had found each other they would never lose each other again. Soul mates indeed!

From my spirit guides I have learned of planes and spheres of being that exist beyond our everyday lives. As discussed in Chapter 2, there are seven levels of these planes and spheres. When we pass from our earthly bodies, we go to one of the seven planes on the other side. The plane that a particular soul will choose to enter depends upon its spiritual progress while in an earthly body.

Those who are not evolved spiritually will choose the first plane where they are able to acquire the knowledge that will help them progress in their journey. Those who have already absorbed knowledge from the first plane will go on to the second plane, then the third, and so on. We progress from plane to plane through our journey to eternity until we perfect ourselves. This is when we have evolved to our highest point—the seventh plane—and we create our existence within the planes. The seventh plane is our eternal home and there we return to the Supreme Being.

Of course it is possible for us to evolve spiritually while we exist in an earthly body. This will come through meditation, through the seeking of truth and knowledge, through listening to your heart, and through finding inner peace. It also comes through giving love to the world around you. The more you give, the more you grow spiritually.

What happens to us when we die? This is a question I am often asked and here is a summary of what I have gleaned from twenty-four years of communicating with the spirits of people who have passed on to another level of existence.

Once a soul is ready to leave the earthly life it must undergo a journey to the next sphere of its existence. Many spirits have told psychically how they were prepared by their guardian angels for their forthcoming journey to the next world. People in a coma may be given glimpses of the world beyond ours, and if they are meant to exit our world they will receive information and instruction while in the comatose state. This removes some of the fear and without fear they do not resist the journey they will soon be taking. Often children who are very sick and close to death are given glimpses of the afterlife and can 'see' and 'hear' their angels around them. Many are able to communicate with their angels and to receive love from the angelic world. When the moment comes for the journey to begin to the other side, at least two angels and some spirit guides arrive to accompany the soul on its journey to the next world.

The spirit guides are usually souls which the traveller can recognise. They are usually relatives or close friends who have already passed over.

The angels will often carry the soul through a tunnel-like structure to the world beyond ours—or if one wishes then the soul can make the journey without being carried. I once had an out-of-body experience where I travelled through the 'tunnel' alone. I wrote about this in Chapter 1. However, most souls are accompanied to the other side. It is there that souls are met by other loved ones whom they recognise. From here the angels allow the loved ones to welcome the newcomer to the next world and to introduce them to their new surroundings.

If a soul has severely suffered before passing over by being very ill or if they are traumatised by an accident and the soul is in shock then they will most likely go to the recovery halls, which are similar to our hospital recovery rooms. Here they can rest and recuperate until they are ready to progress to more learning in their new home.

The soul does in fact have a memory, and we do take events and conversations with us when we pass over. We carry with us who we are in this life into the next. Sometimes it's difficult for us to believe that we still exist after we die. This is not surprising because from early childhood most of us are taught that there is no other life which exists beyond our deaths, and so we become attached to life on earth, to all we can physically see or experience.

We do, however, take everything from this life into the next, and as we learn more here on earth about truth and spirituality, so we also learn and grow more after our physical body dies. This has been reinforced to me not only by my personal experiences and those of my clients, but also by the many other psychics who have been able to receive messages from those who have passed to the other side.

A most joyful and rewarding part of my work involves connecting people with the souls of their loved ones on the other side. One such experience was with a client called Dawn.

The moment I met her I knew that Dawn was feeling depressed because, even though the day was sunny and bright, she seemed to bring an air of dullness and gloom with her.

As our first session began, I soon realised my feelings about Dawn were accurate. She told me she was deeply disturbed by the loss of her daughter, Louisa. Dawn had adopted the baby girl, who was Korean by birth, and sadly she died of Sudden Infant Death Syndrome. Then, a few months after this tragedy, Dawn's mother Enid died as well.

However, the fact that Dawn's losses had occurred some ten years previously led me to be very concerned. Dawn needed help to move on from her grief so that she could enjoy her life. She needed to know that her mother and her daughter were safe and happy.

When I 'tuned in' for Dawn, I immediately felt the presence of the baby's soul. Louisa had many messages for her mother. She wanted Dawn to know that she remembered happy times. She told me about a time when they went to the holiday house and she played with David, the boy next door, and Danny. Dawn then told me that Danny was Louisa's brother and that Dawn had a video of this experience, the last taken of Louisa before she died.

Louisa then said, 'I saw you at the supermarket when the trolley ran away with the baby.' This made no sense to me but Dawn explained that the incident had indeed occurred and her second daughter Hannah, a baby at the time, was in the trolley. Louisa went on to tell her mother that she was often with Hannah in her bedroom, with the light-coloured bedspread, where she read a lot of interesting books and played with Hannah's tape recorder. Dawn confirmed that the description of Hannah's bedroom and her activities were accurate. Louisa also told Dawn to buy a new sewing machine, as her old one was not fixed even though it had recently been repaired.

Enid, Dawn's mother, also appeared and she talked of the house where she had died being demolished and the fact that this pleased her. Dawn explained to me later that her mother never liked the old cottage. Enid also said that she was pleased that Dawn was no longer married to George, who had been abusive. Enid added that she was not happy with the fact that the doctor had not diagnosed her cancer until too late.

As the session progressed, Dawn became aware that her loved ones on the other side were peaceful and happy, and I witnessed a visible change in her. Dawn's recognition of the fact that life continues after death soothed and calmed her, and I saw the depression and anxiety that she had carried with her for so long being replaced by insight and understanding. Now that she had proof that her loved ones lived on happily in the world of spirit, she would be able to let go of her own pain and grief, and be filled with happiness and peace.

I felt that session not only assisted Dawn to heal spiritually, but it also freed the spirits of Enid and Louisa from Dawn's grieving. Sometimes, if we grieve too long for a loved one, it can stop the progression of their spirit on the other side. The bond between souls on earth and spirit souls is very strong when the love between them is strong. Psychically it is like a band of ribbon or elastic joining them. If the earthly soul hangs on to grief for too long, then the band of ribbon may begin to weaken but the spirit of the departed remains here, unable to progress until we release them.

Love and understanding are very powerful energies. If we truly love someone, alive or dead, then we need to let them go, to be free to be whatever they need to be. The love we feel for them will not change. The ribbon keeps our souls connected. By letting go of her grief, Dawn could look forward to peace, inner contentment and the rest of her life, and also be strengthened by the knowledge that she is assisting the spirits of her beloved daughter and mother to be free and to move forward on their own journeys.

Whenever a loving relationship occurs here on earth, the care and concern for the wellbeing of the person we love continues to exist when the body dies and the soul passes over. This is especially true in close family relationships. Love and caring don't end in death.

The experience of Julia, one of my clients, demonstrates how caring continues even when a soul has passed over to the other side. Julia, a school principal, had an interest in spirituality and was fascinated by the idea of being able to access souls who had passed on. She was really missing her mother, Mary, who had died two years previously and whom she loved very much. As we settled in for our first session, Julia was eager to see what would eventuate.

It wasn't long before a lovely, gentle soul appeared before me. The spirit identified herself as Mary and she had come to speak with her daughter. Mary talked of her family and her love of music. She said she had severe problems with her legs and could not walk at the time of her death, which Julia confirmed. Mary also said she remembered how her grandson was playing with a toy train in the room where she lay before she died, a recollection which gave Julia much joy. She talked of dying and described how two angels had carried her ever so gently to the other side. Mary wanted her daughter to know that all was well with her and her spirit was in a beautiful place. She also wanted Julia to know she loved her family and was often with them.

However, our visitor had another important message. Mary told Julia that she was concerned that her husband, who lived alone in a nearby city, was not eating enough. With this Julia started crying and told me it was true and she had been very worried about her father. 'I'm always driving there to fill up his cupboards,' she said. 'But he won't eat.' Mary suggested that it was time to call in a home-care service so that her husband could have some much-needed support.

Although she had journeyed to another plane, Julia's mother clearly demonstrated her care and concern for her husband who was still alive. The love Mary had for her family while she was here on earth remained active even when she became a spirit, a great comfort to those she left behind.

Sometimes when a spirit visits me to pass on information, that spirit can choose to appear in different forms. Some spirits can appear in the same body that they had when they passed over to the next realm. If someone is elderly when they die, they may choose to appear before me in an older form. However, I have learned that even if a person was elderly when they passed over, they don't necessarily have to choose that age in which to appear. Spirits can appear in youthful bodies, even if the person died in old age. Occasionally in my sessions, a spirit may even identify itself to the client by appearing as it looked in a photograph which the client will recognise as I describe what I am seeing.

Some spirits will appear only as light forms. This happened in a session I had with a couple, Tom and Mary, who had lost their only daughter, Lorraine, two months previously in a car accident. She was eighteen years old. Tom and Mary were experiencing the deepest sorrow, and they were driving for two days from another state to see me, in the hope of connecting with their loved one.

When they arrived for their appointment, I was surprised to see how young the couple were themselves. They looked sad, yet somehow hopeful. We spent a few minutes getting to know each other and then Mary proudly showed me three photographs of her beautiful daughter. I immediately felt a deep empathy for Mary and Tom's loss and suffering.

Tom and Mary had asked if they could record the session so I turned on the tape recorder and then told my guests to relax. As soon as I closed my eyes to access the 'communication channel', Lorraine appeared as a lovely clear light.

I had been given no details about Lorraine's death from Tom and Mary, but Lorraine's spirit, in the form of pure light, told me what I needed to know. I heard a sweet voice tell me she was concerned about her friend who was with her in the car accident. Tony was still in a coma and was suffering from brain damage. Lorraine's parents confirmed this—it had been two months since the night of the accident and Tony had not regained consciousness. Lorraine also said she often visited him in the hospital in spirit form.

Lorraine spoke of one of her other friends, saying that she wasn't coping with her death at all. Lorraine asked her mother to give this friend, Cheryl, a photo of her and this would help the girl to let go of some of her pain.

Lorraine then spoke about the pet rabbit she had when she was very young. 'I loved that rabbit,' she said. 'I also love my dog and my cat. I often appear in front of the dog and he can see me.'

Lorraine talked with excitement about her lovely bedroom which she had decorated with new pink curtains shortly before her death. She told us of her favourite wooden toys and asked her father to take them out of the garage and put them in her bedroom as she would have done had she been alive.

She told us how she loves to visit the special spot in the garden where 'the aster flowers grow'. Mary explained that she and Tom had planted asters in a lovely garden bed in the backyard and sprinkled their daughter's ashes there.

Lorraine also expressed concern for her grandmother, Mary's mother, who she said was not well and needed some extra love and attention as the death of her grand-daughter had upset her greatly.

'Ask her if she's all right,' said Tom eagerly.

I put the question to the lovely light and she aswered very brightly, 'I'm fine.'

Lorraine then went on to explain how she 'crossed with the angels'. She said she knew exactly what was happening the whole time, even though everything had gone black just before the impact of the car accident, and she had felt no pain. She explained how one angel had carried her to the other side in her arms, while a second angel was beside her for the whole journey. She described the colours of her new world as being unbelievably bright and beautiful. Lorraine assured her parents that she was very happy and well. 'I wouldn't return to earth even if I could,' she said.

The session continued for an hour and a half, which was unusually long for me. However, it allowed Lorraine and her parents to express their continuing love for each other. She also had another very important message for Tom and Mary.

'I'm looking forward to having the new baby in the family,' she said.

Tom grabbed his wife's hand. 'That's amazing,' he said.

'We have been discussing having another baby to help us get over Lorraine's death.'

Lorraine then told them that they will have a new baby girl. 'She's over here waiting to be born to you.' She said it would happen in about six months, and Mary would have to go into hospital before she could conceive. Mary later explained that she would need a reversal of a tubal ligation operation in order to conceive and that her doctor had given her a good chance of success.

It is unbelievably joyful when a message delivered by a spirit from the other side is proven to be true. And this was exactly what happened with Lorraine. The predictions she made about her parents having a baby girl were correct.

So how did Lorraine's spirit know that this would happen? I believe that she knew because spirits on the other side have access to all information past, present and future. Except that on the other side *there is no past, present and future*—all things just *are.* As such, all information simply exists and can be seen and known by spirits.

Any of this information can be relayed to souls here on earth who may seek it, or who will benefit by such knowledge. This is so in the case of Lorraine, who informed her parents of their forthcoming baby. Not only did this news give them hope, it helped Tom and Mary to lessen their grief for

Lorraine, and also released Lorraine's spirit from the grief of her parents.

The death of a child is something we all find hard to come to terms with when we look at it from a purely physical perspective. However, when we can look more widely, we see things differently, we see more of the universal pattern. Then we learn that even in death our children are not lost to us.

Having been privileged to partake in many discussions between parents and their departed children, it is obvious to me that the bond of love that exists remains the same after death. More than this, the level of awareness that the child's spirit has, even if it was a baby when it died, is extraordinary. Indeed, babies or children who have passed over seem to have an elevated understanding about life on our side, which defies their physical age. This was certainly the case with toddler Charles.

Six years ago, a lovely young couple, Kevin and Katrina, came to see me. The couple also brought their eighteen-month-old baby boy, Joesph, but the reason for their visit was their other son Charles who had died at the age of three.

We settled in and, with the tape recorder running, and baby Joseph secure in his father's arms, the session began. Immediately, I sensed the family was planning to move house but that Kevin was uncertain about it. I sensed that Kevin felt there were too many things wrong with the house they had planned to move into. Then I received a very strong message that the move to this other house would be a positive step. It was from Charles's spirit.

In that session, Charles told us that he had been very frightened before he died, because he knew what was happening with the operation he had to undergo, even though there was no pain and he didn't suffer, and he knew how much his parents loved him. He understood he was not to be on earth for long, as it was part of his journey and the experience was necessary in order for him to progress spiritually.

He explained how there were warning signs that all wasn't well while Katrina was pregnant with him, which she confirmed was true. Charles said he understood everything that happened and he knows the doctor was in error. He was happy they chose a different doctor for the new baby. He said that Katrina blamed herself, but she shouldn't, because she didn't contribute to his death in any way, and it was the very rare heart condition that took him. 'It was intended,' he wanted her to know.

After the operation, Charles said, he knows he slept for a long, long time. He told us that he saw the nurses and knows that one nurse knitted him a little bed cover. He also knew there was a delay with the funeral because it was Easter, and he wanted Katrina to know she shouldn't feel bad about it, as he was already at peace. Charles then told us that he was carried over by an angel, and he saw his grandfather on the other side waiting for him.

Charles then went on to talk about his grandmother who lives in another country. Katrina said that was Kevin's mum who lived in England. Charles knew that Kevin was very sad that his mother didn't see him while he was alive, but he wanted to assure his father that he was often with her now, and they are bonded. However, he advised his parents, he knew that Kevin's mother didn't know how to deal with her loss, and that she should come from England for a visit. Kevin agreed that she wanted to come and they would make it happen soon.

Charles also spoke about Katrina's close friend and how he was often with her two children in spirit and they all spent a lot of time together, which he was part of, and enjoyed.

He then told his parents that they were going to have a daughter, and that they already know each other in spirit on the other side. He said they would have a very rich life ahead of them. He also advised Katrina not to take the job she went for last week, as she would need her energy for her new baby.

Towards the end of the session, Charles gave me a message which I had trouble understanding. He showed me a little school in the country in England. Then Kevin explained that he had visited the school last year because it was his father's school and he wanted to see it. Charles wanted Kevin to know he was with him there.

He also wanted his parents to take his ashes, which were still in their home, to England. 'That's where I want to be,' he said. 'That's where my roots are. That's my heritage.'

Isn't it interesting that souls who pass over as children, or even babies, are able to know things beyond the level of awareness they had while in their earthly bodies?

I found it quite amazing that Charles was able to communicate the complexities of his illness and spiritual journey. He could advise his parents on their best path to dealing with the loss of their son, and was also connected with his grandparents whom he'd never met.

Spirits have access to unlimited knowledge. They are able to relay messages to us about events that have happened in our earthly past and they can communicate to us experiences we are currently undergoing as well as being able to foretell the future. This then makes us wonder about time and our interpretation of it. If spirits can accurately tap into our lives and can tell us about things that have happened, are happening and will happen, what is real time and what is not?

I also find it interesting that the spirits of children who have passed over, like Charles, still need to associate with the spirits of other children, whether their friends are still alive here on earth or are spirits themselves. It makes me wonder when children say that they are playing with an imaginary friend, who they are playing with.

Sometimes a spirit will connect with a loved one on this side to correct a misinterpretation about their death. This can happen in the case of accidental death or suicide. The spirit wants the truth to be known about how, and why, they died. In many of these cases, the spirit comes forward because they want to relieve the suffering of those left behind.

Julie was a high school teacher at a correspondence school. She had felt a strong urge to see me and didn't quite know why as she had never considered going to a psychic before. Once she had settled into our meeting, I asked her if there was anything she would like me to focus on. She answered, rather vaguely, that she just wanted to know if I could tell her anything about anyone who had passed over.

Admittedly, I began to wonder whether I would be able to fill in the hour, until I became aware of the strong presence of a handsome young man with blond hair and lovely tanned skin. He was standing beside Julie in spirit form.

'Who is the young man with the fair hair who died in an accident?' I asked.

'That's Peter,' said Julie as her eyes filled with tears. 'He was my boyfriend.' Then she added in a whisper that he had committed suicide six years ago.

Peter wanted to tell Julie how sorry he was that his death had made her so unhappy. He admitted he had felt unable to cope with life, he particularly hated trying to succeed in a business world in which he didn't belong, and he wanted to assure her that none of his sadness had been her fault. He truly loved her, but he needed to continue his spiritual journey so he could learn to handle his life problems in a different way.

Peter also said he was concerned about his sister, Karen, who had taken his death badly. He knew she was still undergoing therapy, so many years later, to deal with the shock of losing him so suddenly. He spoke of the love he had for Karen, and for his parents. He said he still visited the house in the country where his parents lived.

Then to my surprise, he said, 'I am with our son.'

Julie's eyes opened wide in amazement. She explained that she had lost a child before it was born, and she was very glad to know that he was with Peter.

Towards the end of the session, Peter's spirit faded back to let another spirit talk to Julie. Her grandfather, Arthur, appeared and he simply wanted everyone to know that he was not in limbo. I was puzzled at both Arthur's appearance and message until Julie explained that Arthur had been an atheist while he was alive and the family had always worried that his soul would be in limbo.

But before Julie left, Peter had another message for her, though it took me some time to decipher it.

'Don't forget about Rose,' I heard his voice say. I repeated this for Julie, but she didn't understand.

'Who is Rose?' I asked.

The voice replied, 'Not Rose—roses.'

'Oh,' I laughed, 'roses. He's talking about roses. You placed four of them on his coffin.'

Julie then explained the special message. 'Peter always gave me yellow roses to tell me he loved me,' she said. 'Yellow roses had special meaning for us. I put four yellow roses on Peter's coffin.'

Peter's spirit had orchestrated the session because he wanted Julie to understand the truth about his death so that she could progress with her life. He also wanted to reinforce his love for Julie, and his family, and for them to know that he was at last at peace.

Another point of interest which arose in the story of Peter and Julie is Arthur, the atheist. His family had been concerned that his atheism would mean he was in limbo when he passed over to the other side. However, as Arthur proved, the fact that a person is an atheist while alive does not hinder the soul on the other side. Every soul will find its own level of understanding, on the appropriate plane, as well as the right teachers who will guide their learning and spiritual progress.

However, by seeking the universal truths while alive on earth, we can speed up this process.

This applies to souls who have died as a result of suicide. If you are human and alive then you are sure to undergo suffering from time to time. We all experience suffering in our own ways. Some forms of suffering are part of a group situation. Some people are without food and shelter, or are innocent victims of war. People who are physically, mentally or emotionally handicapped have their own difficulties as well, and so the list goes on.

Suffering is so individualised, so personal, that it is unique to the person experiencing it. What may seem to you a situation without pain and suffering may be a totally different experience for the person involved in that situation. Let me explain what I mean.

Patricia was a lady in her early fifties who came to see me a few months ago after her son, Malcolm, had committed suicide. When Patricia rang to make the appointment, she briefly told me of the circumstances leading to her decision to come to talk with me. Malcolm was only twenty-four years old when he took his life. Patricia had sent him to an exclusive boys' school, believing that he would receive the very best that education had to offer. It was with absolute love in their hearts that she and her husband had made this decision.

Patricia had never noticed any problems with her son as he was growing up. He seemed to be the best son any parent could have. Malcolm was reliable, always contributed to the family and appeared to be handling life really well. At school he did reasonably well in class and had lots of friends whom Patricia always welcomed to her home.

It was therefore a terrible shock when one day Patricia learned that her son had taken his own life. She was devastated—utterly and completely unable to understand why this had happened. After the funeral, Patricia decided to go through Malcolm's personal items to sort them out so that she could feel close to him and keep his room neat and tidy as he would want.

While thumbing through some of Malcolm's old school diaries, Patricia noticed some bizarre drawings, which her son had drawn when he was about sixteen years old. The drawings were quite startling and depicted a great deal of suffering, pain and hurt. Some words had been printed in large letters alongside these drawings, which shook Patricia and her husband Bill to the core. As they searched through Malcolm's books they discovered even more evidence of the suffering that he had clearly endured throughout his school years.

When they put it all together there was only one conclusion they could draw and that was that their much-loved son had been sexually abused for many years by one of his teachers.

They were devastated beyond words. Patricia searched for answers. She believed that Malcolm's death was her fault, because she had been unable to see her son's agony as he was growing up. She felt guilty and believed she had failed as a mother. She cried and cried as we talked, saying that she had been a terrible mother.

As she sobbed I asked for guidance. My prayer was soon answered. I found myself uttering words of comfort, encouragement, love and insight into Patricia's trauma. We were told that Malcolm was safe and happy on the other side, and that he definitely did not want to return to earth where he had suffered so much. He spoke of his love for his mum and dad, and for his sister with whom he had been close. He asked that his mum and dad try to stop grieving, especially as he was pleased that his unhappy life was at an end.

Patricia began to settle down as she listened to the messages of love and encouragement from her beloved son. I told her quite firmly that nothing is given to us that we are not equipped to handle, and assured her that she was a very strong lady and that she could come to terms with her son's death. As time passed I could feel the pain of Patricia's hurt gradually diminishing.

Finally, it became quite dark in the room where we were. I knew that Patricia had a long drive home ahead of her so I stood up and gave her a big hug as I assured her that she would certainly begin to feel better soon. I knew that she would continue to grieve, but with more of an understanding of her son's pain and with less guilt for herself.

The sadness Patricia felt was made up of the normal grief a mother feels when her child passes on and the grief she felt when she first discovered that her son had been abused by a teacher at his school. This grief had been compounded by a sense of failure and guilt, because she and her husband had not known that their boy had been suffering from the trauma of the abuse he had experienced.

Patricia's reading helped her to recognise that she had not failed her son, that she was a wonderful, loving mother, and that her son truly appreciated his wonderful family and was grateful for all the love they had given him.

Recently, Patricia phoned me to make an appointment to come and have another talk about her son. She was still suffering, but every day she was gradually letting go of her own agony and remembering that she was truly equipped to handle such incredible torment. When she does come to see me, I'll remind her again that her love for her son will always continue, but that her pain and suffering will certainly diminish.

Isn't it wonderful to know that our love for each other continues on beyond the veil of death and that true love is a bond so strong that we can never be separated from our loved ones? We can therefore see that death need hold no fear for us. We are surrounded by love and angels in death. We are guided and led along the way and we will reconnect with our loved ones on the other side.

As we grow and learn here on earth so we will grow and learn on the other side. We can manifest whatever we wish there. We can choose the type of existence we wish as long as we are growing spiritually from the choices we make. We will have guardians and teachers there just as we do here, and we will make decisions there about our future existence, which could include choosing another life on earth or maybe not, depending on who we are, how evolved we are and what is best for our overall growth.

4

Have we lived before?

I believe we do come to earth over and over again to perfect our learning, and that we have many lives both here and on other planes. This is necessary for us to progress at every level of our consciousness and for the growth of our souls as we journey to eternity.

I believe when we leave this earthly body, we journey to another plane of existence where our spirit is nurtured and trained in order to prepare us for our return to earth. We come back in order to learn the lessons that we did not successfully master during our previous lives. We spend many lifetimes perfecting our souls as we make our journey through existence. Earth is the arena where we face situations which challenge us and where we grow spiritually. We learn our lessons on earth and then travel on to the spiritual realm in between earthly lives. We remain there, learning as much as we can, until we decide to reincarnate to earth. This cycle continues on until we no longer need to reincarnate because we have perfected our soul. When finally this happens, we remain in the realm of the Supreme Being for all eternity.

Many people ask me to tell them about their past lives. Although I prefer to help a person to deal with their present existence, I do find the opportunity to discover more about the soul's journey very rewarding. Also, as you will see from this chapter, our past lives can actively participate in our present, and insight into them can tell us a lot about who we really are. That said, it is still more important to deal with current issues before taking on our past. We should always remember that we are here, in this life, and now is the time we must learn and grow as much as we can.

Sometimes when people have a past-life reading, they are told by the medium conducting the session that they had been someone great, a leader or king or queen, or some other famous historical figure. I quite happily admit I have not yet encountered such a prestigious soul within a client; however, this does not necessarily mean that Cleopatra or Henry VIII has not reincarnated into the body of a person who is now living amongst us. It simply means I haven't met such a person in this lifetime so far.

Fortunately for me, my clients have all been philosophical about having a past life in which they were ordinary people, each progressing on their spiritual journey, and most have a sense of humour about not having been a famous person in the past.

So, how do I 'see' people's past lives? Whenever I tune in to a soul and receive messages about past lives, it is much like watching a movie or flicking through a picture book of that person's entire existence. This information is given directly from spirit guides and angels who dwell in the spiritual realm. I may be shown images of their present, future or past lives, depending on the message. I can psychically 'scan' the person's soul memory, which is like a blueprint of who they are and everything they have experienced.

The soul memory retains all the events, experiences, knowledge and truths, both positive and negative, that the soul has ever encountered. The memory of all events is locked into the soul and it is from these files that a psychic can read information.

We often reincarnate with other souls that we have been with in previous lifetimes. We have all met people that we feel instantly connected to, and sometimes we intuitively feel that we know them well. This feeling may also happen when we visit places we have never been before. This could well be due to the fact that we have lived there in another lifetime.

So people can develop a deep bond with others and with other places in the world which defies a logical explanation. That is because the connection is from the spiritual realm—we could have met in a past life.

While I can do a reading specifically to look into past lives, this isn't necessarily what I'll see. Our guides will only show us what is good and right for us, and sometimes, if it's not appropriate, I won't be shown a past life at all—even if strongly requested!

An experienced psychic is able to tap into a person's soul memory; however, not every medium will be shown the same past life for a particular person. Sometimes, though, this does occur, and it reminds us of the very real connection we have with the world of spirit.

One such occasion was a reading I did for my client Brian who lives alone in a lovely country town by the ocean in New South Wales. Brian is a very busy young business executive, who lives a hectic but fulfilling life. He came to see me one day while he was visiting the city. He had heard about my work and he hoped I might be able to assist him with some business decisions that he needed to make.

During the session, I focused on some choices that Brian could make concerning his business, when he suddenly asked me if I ever looked into past lives. I was surprised, as so far most of the session had concerned Brian's current life, but was pleased to look into his soul's past.

I was shown a scene in a French court. I could see that it was an extremely extravagant era in history, with mirrors and paintings adorning the long halls of an opulent palace. Men and women, all richly dressed and adorned with hair wigs and facial make-up, were assembled in a vast hall, busily socialising.

Suddenly, I recognised my client. He looked very much like he does in his present life, except that in my vision he was dressed in the clothes of the era, with blue breeches and a white wig, which rather suited his handsome face. He had the air of a man with a mission, and in fact he was a very important man in that lifetime — an emissary of the king. He had arrived at the court after delivering an important message from the king to the ruler of another country, and his return was being celebrated by the people assembled in the hall.

I heard the young man's name was Claude. When I repeated this information for Brian, he looked at me with eyes wide open and mouth agape. 'That is unbelievable,' he gasped.

Of course I wanted to know why that was so unbelievable. To my question Brian replied that he had a friend who also lived in the country near him. This friend, Paul, also had psychic gifts. Sometimes they would get together for a meal and usually psychic matters would become the topic of conversation. Brian then went on to say that Paul could also see into past lives, and that he had seen the same life in which Brian had been an emissary in a court in France and that his name was Claude.

Learning about our past lives can help us to better understand our lives here and now, as long as we always focus on the present. I have a wonderful friend called Maree who lives in country New South Wales with her husband Jerry. I am fortunate enough to be able to stay at their home from time to time. On one visit, Maree and I were having our usual after-dinner chat in the lounge room by the warm potbelly stove when Maree asked if I could do a past-life reading for her. I was as inquisitive as she about her soul, so I tuned in.

I was soon shown a very sad and lonely female figure standing by a lake in Ireland. It was Maree in another lifetime. She had deserted her family. She had walked away from nine children and a husband who needed her. Their life had been very hard and there was never enough money to buy the food or clothing that the family needed. The woman had struggled and tried to be a good wife and mother, only to find each day longer and harder than the day before, until finally one day she could no longer face the suffering of her children and her abusive husband, and she simply walked away from the house, taking nothing with her. The woman had stopped beside the lake and, as she stood on the icy shore, the deep waters became more and more enticing until she surrendered to her desperate circumstances and dived in and drowned. And while Maree's soul found peace on the other side, as her angels received her, she would regret that decision for many lifetimes to come.

My friend Maree was devastated to have been this woman. Maree is the proud mother of five delightful children and, not only are they economically secure, but Maree strives very hard to be the best mother any child could have. At first Maree protested that it couldn't have been her, because in this life there was nothing more important to her than her beautiful family and no matter what happened she could never abandon them.

However, Maree soon gained a clearer understanding that in this lifetime she was actually fulfilling her destiny by devoting herself to her children and husband. Maree also later said that the experience of her past life helped to explain why she was sometimes overprotective of her children—she wasn't going to lose them again.

Often we can obtain a clearer picture of who we really are when we see who we were in a past-life existence. This is so with Arlene, who decided to have a psychic session with me to reveal her past to her.

When the appointed time arrived, I was delighted to greet Arlene and usher her into the consulting room up the stairs in our light and airy home. Arlene was a very attractive lady, tall and slim with dark hair and honest eyes. She asked me if I would kindly give her a psychic review of her health. As we proceeded with the session, it became clear that she was recovering from that all too common major illness—cancer.

In Arlene's case, the cancer had been in the bowel and she was mercifully clear of the problem now, and had been for some months. As I suggested to her certain vitamins, minerals and herbs that would assist to protect and strengthen her, I 'picked up' that Arlene had a teenage daughter. She beamed as I told her I could see that her daughter and she were very, very close.

'We do have a very strong bond,' said Arlene, 'sometimes it seems almost abnormal.' We discussed this situation a little further and soon our session was out of time. Arlene thanked me warmly and happily told me that she would return one day to find out whatever we could about the relationship between herself and her daughter, Chloe.

I was pleased when Arlene once again visited me for a session. This visit, she wanted to spend the time exploring the bond between herself and her daughter. As I tuned in to try to find out why Arlene and her daughter were so unusually close, I began to find myself slowly travelling into a past life.

I could see that Arlene and Chloe were living in Europe in the early 1800s. I just 'knew' that this was the timeframe in which they lived, and as I scanned the scene in front of my psychic eye I could see that Arlene was a young and handsome man. Her daughter Chloe was a small female child, and the pair were dressed in costumes applicable to the age in which they lived.

Arlene, then a young man, was dressed in ragged trousers and a rather once ornate billowing shirt. I could see that he had obviously come from a wealthy background, but for some reason his good fortune was not now evident.

So it was with Chloe. As the little girl, I could see that she wore a once pretty gown made of lots of beautiful fabric and decorated with lace and ribbon. However, the scene in front of my eyes was certainly not a happy one. The little girl was sobbing slowly and deeply as she held out her arms to the young man. He too was obviously very upset as he reached out to meet the girl's arms. As they embraced I knew that this embrace was in fact a signal of the parting that was very soon to take place between them.

Sure enough, the young man held the little girl in his arms and she clung tightly onto him. Next, he held her quite suddenly at arm's length and very quickly and deliberately he turned away from her. She screamed out for him to come back as he raced faster and faster away from her. By then many people had crowded into the scene before my eyes, and soon the young man was pushing his way through the crowd getting further and further away from the crying, screaming young girl.

As I watched I saw that the girl collapsed onto the cobbled path on which she sat, and the young man was swallowed up by the crowd. I knew that the pair were brother and sister. So Arlene and Chloe had been brother and sister.

As I tuned in more deeply to the scene I realised that the young man had decided to leave his sister to go out into the world and try to find food, clothing and shelter for her. I knew too that there were two more children in the family, but I was unable to see where they were.

I knew that the house in which the family had previously lived with their parents had been burned down. The parents had died in the massive fire that had raged through their expensive home. The love between the siblings was extremely obvious, and I knew that the young man had no choice but to go off to find food and shelter for his sister. It really hurt him to leave her behind on the street, but he hoped he would be back soon to protect and look after her. The scene faded quickly before my eyes as I returned to the room where Arlene was sitting in front of me with a dazed look of disbelief.

I explained to her that she and Chloe were close in this life because they had made a pact between them to be together and never to let each other go in their next reincarnation. Here they were now, mother and daughter, both strongly loving and protecting each other with a bond that no event in life could ever sever. Arlene cried as I told her of this bond and why it was so strong. She thanked me for the information I had given her, and booked another appointment with me, hoping that more of the jigsaw of her life might be made clearer to her.

One of the reasons why a past-life reading can be beneficial is that it can show people why certain problems may be occurring in their present life, and therefore healing can be achieved more efficiently. Often our fears and phobias are rooted in our past lives and there is a valid reason why we may be scared of snakes or have a fear of water; we may have died in a past life as a result of a snake bite or from drowning.

Our soul memories, where we file all our experiences from our past lives, are strongly embedded in our consciousness in this lifetime. This can affect us dramatically, as was the case with Jean, who asked if I could help her to understand why she had a fear of heights.

Jean told me her fear prevented her from walking up a flight of stairs, let alone sitting in a chairlift or climbing a steep incline. She could not go anywhere where height was involved. She told me that even in the movie theatres she had to sit in the lower sections, otherwise she would be overtaken by fear and not enjoy the movie. Jean was a lovely person and I felt immediately sad that she was suffering so extensively from this problem.

Jean's reading revealed that in a past life she had been a very wealthy young lady of high social standing. She appeared before me dressed in a magnificent gown of white embossed satin, beautifully embroidered with pink roses. She was gorgeous and had the world at her feet.

As the scene progressed, I saw the beautiful lady travelling across country in a horse-drawn coach. There were also three or four other coaches, all travelling in the same direction. Suddenly the white horses that were pulling the lady's coach began to bolt, and as they galloped faster and faster the coach picked up more and more speed.

The young lady inside the coach became very frightened as she realised what was happening. But the horses were completely out of control, and no matter how hard the driver and coachmen tried, they were unable to stop them and they bolted on to a narrow, winding track which followed the rugged coastline high above the raging sea.

Then I saw the carriage become unhinged from the wooden shafts which attached it to the horses' harness. The carriage tumbled to the ground and hurtled over the cliff, taking the lady to her death.

The experience of falling ever faster and knowing that she could do nothing to save herself was embedded in Jean's soul memory and was so strong that it greatly affected her present life. At the end of the session, Jean was both relieved, that there was in fact an explanation as to why she could not manage heights, and sad because of the tragic death she had had to endure in that previous lifetime.

Jean telephoned a couple of months later to tell me that she no longer felt inadequate because of her fear of heights. She said her attitude had changed completely, and she now understood her fear and accepted that it was fine for her to have this problem. She felt confident that now she knew the reason for her fear, she could work at overcoming it.

If you have a burning ambition to do a particular thing or to live a certain life, and even if your current life does not accommodate this dream, then chances are that your ambition comes from deep within your soul memory. In this way, the past and present can merge, and in doing so fulfil our ambitions and destiny.

Such was the case with Maureen, who came to see me for a general reading in the hope of finding some insight into her life. Though content with her life, Maureen felt that she lacked direction and that something was missing. Her first session proved to be most revealing. She had been given many spiritual issues to deal with in this lifetime and many challenges to overcome. We discussed these, and Maureen told me that the need to help people less fortunate than herself had been a driving force for her since she was a young child.

As I tuned in, I was shown a very sad scene. There was a little girl about six years old, wandering aimlessly along a cobbled street. People were everywhere around her, but no one took any notice of her. She was bedraggled and unkempt, her clothes were streaked with dirt and her hair was straggly. The girl stopped by a garbage bin at the side of the street and fingered through bits of dry bread and vegetable scraps. Eagerly, she scooped up a handful of this into her scrawny little hand and hungrily ate piece after piece of the foul-looking debris.

I felt deeply moved by the vision. Life was extremely hard for this little girl, she was alone in the world and survived by her wits. She struggled to find enough food to sustain her body. I saw that her adolescent years on the streets were even more difficult, even though she had managed to find other homeless children and together they formed into small groups who would go out to beg, steal or scrounge for food.

I was so affected by what I was shown that at first I did not notice Maureen, who was crying with uncontrollable sorrow. She told me that she recognised herself, that she somehow knew that she was the little girl in a previous life.

This insight into her past life explained to Maureen why she had a deep empathy for poor and homeless people, especially children. She told me about her secret aspirations to help homeless kids whose ill-fortune led them to live, as she had done, on the streets. Maureen's life changed in that instant. She made a vow then and there to devote her energy and resources to helping homeless children.

A couple of months later, Maureen phoned to tell me she had become a very busy lady. She now worked with a team of people who delivered food to large numbers of homeless children. Maureen said that every time she handed a warm, appetising meal to a hungry child, her heart swelled with pride and happiness because she understood deeply how happy this simple act made the unfortunate child feel. Maureen told me that at last she felt truly fulfilled.

A similar connection between past and present occurred for my client Wendy. Wendy was about twenty years of age when she came to see me. She wanted to see what the next few years would bring for her, as she had recently finished studying for a degree in primary school teaching and was looking forward to commencing her career as a teacher.

As I connected with her spirit guides, I was told that Wendy would be travelling overseas soon, where she would decide to stay for quite a long period. I saw her living with a family in Scotland, and that the father in that family would be a lawyer and Wendy would be employed as a nanny to the three children. Things would go well for her and she would certainly be happy.

Wendy was delighted with this news. She told me that she had hoped to visit Scotland one day, because she was very interested in all things Scottish, although she wasn't sure why. As if in answer to Wendy's question, her guides then showed me one of Wendy's past lives.

Wendy had lived in Scotland many years ago, and in that life she had been born into a large family of five sons and one daughter, Margaret. The family was wealthy and owned a whiskey distillery near Glasgow. This past life explained why Wendy felt such a strong connection with Scotland in her current life.

A couple of years later, I heard from Wendy again. She told me that she had decided to take a long trip to Europe and the United Kingdom and, as I had predicted, she had settled in Scotland where she answered an advertisement for a nanny in the local paper. Upon arriving at the house to meet the family, Wendy was surprised to find that the father of the family was a lawyer and she would be caring for three children.

Wendy also decided to research her past-life existence. She told me how she went from one library to another in her spare time, looking up record after record until, amazingly, she found a family with one daughter named Margaret and five sons who had been extremely wealthy from money gained through selling whiskey.

However, Wendy's greatest discovery from the entire experience, she said, was her insight. 'I really did have a powerful connection with Scotland,' she said. 'When I arrived there I really felt at home, I just knew I belonged.'

The truth is that we are complex and complicated. There are many layers to our being. We have locked into our souls all the memories—past and present—of our earthly and spiritual realm existences. Recognising who we are and the richness of our past experiences can enhance our lives as we travel towards our final destination—eternity.

5

Guided by angels

Each and every one of us has wonderful, loving, caring spirits around us whose duty is to guard, protect and guide us through our lives. These spirit guides are with us at all times, and so when we need help we must not be afraid to ask for it.

Our guides will always hear us if we ask for help. They will always be willing to give us answers to our questions and to cooperate with us in achieving our goals. However, our guides will never make decisions for us. That responsibility lies with each individual. We are here to learn and grow, so we each have to lead the way in our journeys.

When you get to know your guides, you will always feel safe and protected, and you will be able to soar ahead with confidence as you unlock the secrets of your being. You can get to know your guide by various means. One way is to seek the help of a psychic or clairvoyant to connect you with your guide. Meditation is also of great value if you are seeking access to your guide, though you may need to be patient and persistent with this method. You could also attend a religious service or church because, even if it isn't your particular religion, the spiritual experience can help you tune in to your guides.

As well as helping us to progress on our spiritual journeys, our guides watch over the state of our physical, mental and emotional health. They can send us healing energy, usually through a medium such as a psychic healer.

For example, when I conduct a healing session, I will ask the client's spirit guide for information about the person's health and the best way of dealing with any problems. Sometimes, the guides may advise a specific course of action or treatment, or they may simply warn the client of potential problems. The session is often concluded with the client receiving spiritual healing energy which I collect from their guides and radiate from my hands directly to the client. This energy 'washes' over them, and it is interesting how many people say they can feel heat from my hands even though I never actually touch them.

Throughout our lifetimes we will have many different guides. Particular guides will be with us to deal with the various issues and stages of our lives. For example, if you are studying, you will draw a spirit guide to help you utilise the power of your mind. A first-time mother may have a guide with highly developed nurturing skills, while a mother of three young children may need a guide who gives her lots of energy. If we are dealing with the loss of a loved one, we may find a guide to help us deal with our grief. This also explains why various psychics will see different spirit guides for the same person.

We all have a master guide who stays with us from the very first incarnation to our very last and beyond. These master guides are pure souls without earthly faults in spirit or personality. These guides are fully evolved and may or may not have ever had an existence on earth. They are in charge of all our other guides who come and go within our lifetimes. Our master guide is strongly a part of us, knows us intimately, and is the one we see when we pass from one existence into another. This guide protects us, loves us and is there for us eternally. They have unlimited knowledge and hold all the answers to our spirituality and growth.

Guides can be the spirits of deceased relatives who have chosen to remain closely with us, to give us the benefit of their own growth and learning through the experiences they had both in their own earthly lives and in the spiritual realms. They may be attracted to us for many reasons. Perhaps they had chosen to be in the same earthly family as we ourselves chose, or perhaps they recognised that the values they held in life are similar to the values we ourselves hold.

Recently, a lady named Elizabeth came to see me for guidance about her life. She was more interested in knowing what I saw for her health, her career and her relationships than she was in her guides; however, at the end of her session, she asked if she had any spirits with her.

I immediately saw a dark-haired lady who seemed quiet and kind. There was nurturing and motherliness in her soul. She said her name was Barbara.

When I described the lady to Elizabeth, she replied that Barbara was her grandmother who died twelve years ago. Elizabeth told me how close she had been to Barbara and how her grandmother had lived in the same house as Elizabeth and her family. Elizabeth admitted she thought about Barbara often and still misses her greatly, even now, twelve years later.

It was no surprise then that Barbara was still with Elizabeth, as her spirit guide. And Elizabeth was delighted to know that her grandmother remained very much a part of her life.

Sometimes we can have personality traits that connect us with our spirit guides. If we have a guide who was particularly gifted while they were alive, here on earth, and if we are fortunate enough to inherit some of that gift, then we can reach incredible heights using the combined energy of ourselves and our spirit guides.

My client, Pamela, was one of these fortunate souls with a talented guide. Pamela is a fashion designer who had seen me previously for readings. She is very successful in her business, both here in Australia as well as internationally in Europe, Britain and the United States. Her clothing can be purchased in leading stores throughout the world. For all of her success, however, Pamela remains quite humble and she has a beautiful, loving view on life.

For this particular session, Pamela had brought her husband Grant along for a joint reading of their lives, both as a couple and separately. I was enjoying reading for this happily married couple who seemed so content with their lives, when a lovely dark-haired lady appeared.

The lady guide was very beautiful. She had an air of elegance and style about her, and her energy psychically lit up the whole room with the crystal-like whiteness of her soul. She told me she was European and was related to Pamela.

Pamela confirmed her family was European, but at first she could not recognise the spirit. Then she suddenly exclaimed, 'It's my aunt who died during World War II. She was only twenty-seven when she was put to death by the Nazis. She used to love beautiful things, especially clothes.' Pamela told us that her aunt had been very creative and made all of her own clothes. They were of the finest materials, and she loved to show them off. 'I inherited some of her clothes,' Pamela revealed. 'I was only very young when I got them, but I loved them so much that they inspired me to study dress design and fashion, and that's why I'm now in the fashion industry.'

Pamela had always been sad that her aunt's life was cut short and she had been unable to use her creative gifts fully. However, after that session Pamela realised with great joy that her aunt's gift continued to be expressed—through her. For me it was further confirmation of how our guides enhance and enrich our lives with their wonderful energy.

While I have found that spirit guides are often family members—some of whom are easily recognised and some of whom are not—a guide may also be completely unrelated to the person. This is usually the case with our master guides, but also occurs with other guides. The story of Jason and one of his guides is an interesting example of this. Sometimes I do readings for people who live overseas. I do this by telephone, or by recording the session on a tape which I send to the client and sometimes we will then discuss various aspects of the session.

Jason, a medical practitioner working in a busy East Coast medical centre in the United States, contacted me for one of these long-distance readings. At my request, he sent me a photograph of himself and a tape of him asking me questions.

No sooner had I tuned in to his questions than the information began to flow. I found myself seeing clearly into Jason's soul and the answers to his questions came quickly. Towards the end of Jason's session, I suddenly became aware of the presence of a gentle male spirit. I tried to continue with the messages I was being given, thinking I would come back to the spirit, but he was quite determined to get my attention as he proclaimed that he *was* one of Jason's spirit guides.

'My name is Dr Ehrlich,' he declared, 'and I am Jason's healing guide. I help him with his medical work.' With some surprise, I gave this information to Jason, but somehow I felt unsure about actually naming the guide so I decided not to mention it.

However, the spirit guide interrupted again. 'Please tell Jason that I am the German Dr Ehrlich and that I am his healing guide,' he said.

What else could I do? The spirit was becoming extremely insistent. So I told Jason his spirit guide's name and with that I quickly finished off the session, inviting Jason to contact me if he had any queries or comments concerning the session.

About a week later I received an email from Jason. He said that he was very pleased with his session and requested clarification of a few points I had raised. Jason added that he was a specialist physician in rheumatology, 'a discipline that addresses diseases that result from derangements in immune function'. Jason explained that he was drawn to it because of his 'love for immunology', a medical science that got its start in the early 1900s. 'I well remember my student days, when I studied the pioneering work of the great German bacteriologist Paul Ehrlich, winner of the 1908 Nobel Prize for Medicine,' he said. 'To think he could be my spirit guide is truly awesome.'

I felt delighted for Jason that his spirit guide was so significant in his life. I also felt reinforced in my belief that the information I receive should be delivered with total confidence. Rarely do I doubt myself or the information I receive, nor do I need to have proof of the correctness of this information, however it is wonderful when it happens and I am grateful to have witnessed this many times over many years.

When a master guide appears during a session, I am truly in awe and feel humbled to be in the presence of such a being. Often I might only see their face. Sometimes I see them dressed in clothing which represents the era or culture from which they choose to appear—Indian guides may be dressed in turbans and gaily coloured robes, trousers and tunics; female guides often manifest in magnificent flowing gowns, of silk, chiffon, cotton and satin, or embroidered with intricate patterns, the colours and delicacy of which are breathtakingly beautiful.

The higher guides rarely give me actual messages. They just appear, but sometimes, as I learnt from my experience with my friend Sylvia, the appearance of a master guide *is* the message.

Sylvia, a headmistress of a large school in the inner city, had been coming to see me for many years for a psychic glance into her life. On this particular day, our session was progressing well when I suddenly noticed a monk dressed in a purple hooded robe standing close beside her.

I knew that this spirit was very evolved by the overwhelming peacefulness and extraordinary energy which surrounded him. He didn't speak to Sylvia but his presence made it clear that she was in very loving and protective hands and that she had nothing to fear with this spirit taking care of her. Three weeks later, I received a phone call from Sylvia. She was in hospital, having some exploratory tests to determine the cause of an illness. The following week her illness was diagnosed—bowel cancer—and Sylvia immediately underwent an operation for the removal of a very aggressive tumour in her bowel. Sadly, Sylvia passed away a couple of weeks later.

Apart from the grief of losing a friend, I was shocked as I had certainly not seen any sign of illness during Sylvia's reading, let alone bowel cancer. Then I remembered the monk in purple standing beside her. Was his appearance the message, I wondered.

Now, I believe this experience taught me that before we die, we are assigned a higher spirit to guide us throughout the final stages of our earthly lives and then to take us to the other side. I believe it was intended that Sylvia was unaware of her illness and impending death, and I was not to know of the relevance of the higher guide by her side. If I had known, I could not have coped with the session or Sylvia's illness, because of our friendship.

Our spirit guides know us intimately and have profound effects on each of us throughout our lives and beyond, mostly without us realising that we are indeed being guided. I'm sure most of us can recall occasions when it seemed like we were rescued or protected from some terrible situation, or were suddenly inspired to make a decision that changed our life. Some of us have even miraculously survived accidents or life-threatening illnesses, against all the odds. On occasions like these, we can rest assured that our guides are with us.

Ralph's example shows the far-reaching effect our guides have on our lives, and lifetimes. I liked Ralph from the moment I first met him. He was in his late forties, and youthful-looking except for very tired eyes. Ralph's wife, Rosalie, had seen me a couple of months prior to his visit and during her session I had received messages that Ralph was unwell and needed to take certain herbs and vitamins for more energy. It was no surprise, then, when Ralph later made an appointment to see me for a health reading.

As Ralph's session progressed, I discovered he had not been well for almost a year, and that he had found himself unable to continue with his job as a painter. Ralph told me that over many years he had been affected by the paint fumes and he now suffered from a condition similar to chronic fatigue syndrome. He also had the symptoms of early onset diabetes, which he was controlling with the help of a dietitian. And while he and Rosalie were very happily married, Ralph was feeling depleted in energy and had lost his enthusiasm for life. He was also feeling depressed about his future now that he could no longer work as a painter.

In Ralph's reading, I immediately saw happiness and good health in his future. He found this news hard to believe, though to me the message seemed quite clear. I could see that certain changes to his diet which he was making would benefit him and that he would move to the hills around Byron Bay. Ralph seemed pleased with the information, admitting that he'd always wanted to live in that exact location, but he remained unconvinced of his bright future.

Unfazed by his scepticism, I then moved on to tell Ralph that I saw him importing Native American Indian artefacts, jewellery and handcrafts into Australia. I saw many outlets here, all owned by Ralph, where these beautiful objects would be sold.

Even before I finished telling Ralph what I saw, he was staring at me in disbelief. He seemed so shocked I actually stopped the reading to ask if he was all right. Then Ralph explained that this had always been his secret dream. He had been interested in Native American Indian culture for a long time, and had considered travelling to the United States to visit Indian reservations and learn about the Indian way of life. 'How did you know?' Ralph asked.

I told Ralph I saw a very large image of a male guide who was wearing a white robe with a medallion of some kind around his neck. This guide informed me that Ralph was a very old soul who, in one lifetime, had been an Indian who had tried to develop peace and understanding between the Native American Indians and the 'white men' when they first arrived.

The spirit guide went on to explain that there was much work ahead for Ralph, because in this current lifetime Ralph was to continue his work as a peace-maker, bringing together Native American Indian culture and the West through his new business. The guide hoped that Ralph would see this as valuable work, and that he would experience a great sense of joy and fulfilment in doing this. Ralph's guide also promised to assist in the job of making this all happen.

Ralph left that session a changed man—animated, energetic and with a wonderful new zest for life. I knew that his health would now return to him and that he would be happy and successful on his true path.

Sure enough, about one year later, Ralph called to tell me that he had just returned from the United States where he had learned what he needed to know to set up his business. It was just as his spirit guide had said, and Ralph was now totally convinced of our connections with the spirit world.

Spirit guides are very close to all of us, and even though in the normal course of our lives we do not openly interact with them, much connection is actually taking place between them and us. Our guides are with us at all times. When our lives are good and all seems to be going according to our wishes, our guides are with us. Also, when our lives are difficult, nothing seems to be going right and we're at our lowest, our guides are with us. We always have the support of our guides.

We can always talk to our guides. We can also ask them for help with problems in our lives. However, you should not expect an *instant* response, and for the best results make sure your request is clear and specific. Importantly, remember that while our guides will always assist us, they cannot live our lives for us, and we must each take responsibility for our decisions. Also, do not take your guides for granted—like any other living soul, they respond to our love and our appreciation of them.

Guides communicate with us in many different ways and often these are most unexpected. Be open-minded when you connect with your guide. Messages often come through psychics, who see and hear guides when they tune in to the psychic energy which exists in all realms. However, we can also learn to receive these messages ourselves by trusting our feelings and intuition.

Meditation is a wonderful way to develop your spirituality and your guides will often meet you in this quiet space. Through meditation, your guides can communicate with you as well as shower you with love and peace, and you will develop your own psychic abilities and learn to trust your feelings.

Wisdom comes from within. We will never find more truth anywhere than the truth we each have within ourselves.

We hold all our own answers and we can find them through inner contemplation. Trust yourself that the answers will come from within you. Know that your intuition will *always* be right because it is linked to your spirit guides.

6

Seeking our higher selves

Many times we are tested by the universe as to our courage and strength. Often we take fright and end up veering off our true path, causing us further pain. When we do lose direction and become lost, we need to ask for redirection and take control of our journey through life. First, we need to recognise where we have gone wrong. This might require us letting go of a relationship, changing a career, deciding to have a child or not to have one. Recognising this, we then can take control of our lives, find our way back to the right path and travel along it once more.

Once we have reconnected ourselves to our true path in life we will find we are in tune with ourselves, particularly our higher selves, and with the world around us. Life will then become what we want it to be. There are times when we need to be brave and to use our strength to make the necessary life changes that will get us back on track. We may in fact have to harness a lot of inner strength, strength which may have previously lain dormant within us. If we trust our inner guidance, our gut feelings, our intuition, then we are well on the way to making the right choices for our life's direction. We may even be surprised by how strong we really are.

Many people who come to me for guidance are confused, fearful and unhappy with their lives. Unfortunately, these people have lost touch with the spiritual realm, and their higher selves.

The higher self is finely attuned to the spiritual realm. It is an in-built mechanism that forms part of our soul. It has the knowledge for our highest good, the knowledge that has been stored throughout our many lifetimes here on earth and in other planes of existence. It is our direct link with our guides, and it is the 'self' that stays with us all of our spiritual lives. When you trust your higher self to guide you, you will always make the right decisions.

The lower self, on the other hand, is that part of us which is in tune with our earthly needs. These are the needs that demand to be met as quickly and easily as possible. The lower self is only concerned with this lifetime, as opposed to the higher self which guides our entire spiritual journey, so sometimes it can lead us to make the wrong decisions in our lives. When the lower self takes over from the higher, we forget the real purpose of life and do not progress spiritually.

We all know what it feels like to have major problems in our lives. It's not much fun, and our lower selves will instinctively look for the easiest way out. However, problems are part of earthly life, because this life is simply a testing ground in which we develop our spiritual truth and knowledge, so it's our attitude towards our challenges which makes or breaks us. Our higher self will never let us down in this respect. In fact, when we are faced with challenges our higher self will show us that we have the inner strength and resources to overcome our problems with ease.

When we use our higher selves to deal with life's difficulties, we not only tap into our spiritual strength, we renew that strength, and more than this, we actually increase it. This is what spiritual growth is all about—our journey to our full potential. So while we need not go out of our way to look for problems, when we find ourselves confronted by life's difficulties, we should look at them from a broader perspective—from our higher selves. It's amazing how things will change for us if we practise this simple truth.

Life can be confusing and challenging at times, and we wonder what we're doing here, but we are all very special beings who have come to earth to learn and grow spiritually. If life went smoothly for us all the time and our existence was idyllic, then we would not need to examine ourselves deeply to learn how to cope with our problems. When we are not satisfied with our lives, we are prompted to find answers, to change and to grow spiritually. It is the struggles in our lives that enable us to grow.

When we learn to treat our problems as spiritual challenges, we progress more quickly in our journey to enlightenment. Each time a problem is solved, we will experience a sense of wellbeing and fulfilment—one of the elusive states that we are all searching for. So no matter what the problem is, remember that you are spiritually equipped to handle it.

This was certainly so for Rita. She knew that there was so much more to herself than she was able to recognise. Rita was a busy wife and mother of two lovely children, but she felt that something was strongly missing from her life.

She became very restless and unsettled, and she seemed to be driven by a part of herself that she could not understand. She searched her own mind for answers, but found none. Gradually, her health began to suffer as she became more dissatisfied with her life.

Rita decided to seek psychic advice for answers and as I tuned in to her soul I discovered that indeed there was a whole lot more to her than anyone knew. I saw that Rita was in fact a spiritual master. Her guides revealed themselves to me and I was astonished by their majesty. They appeared in all regalia, one a monsignor of the Roman Catholic church and another a high priest who had lived a life in ancient Egypt.

Through the monsignor Rita learned that she was a very high soul who had a lot of knowledge to share with people in her lifetime. She was told that if she did not connect with her higher self, which housed all this wonderful knowledge, and share her truths with others, then she would continue to feel unfulfilled and empty, just as she had been feeling lately.

Rita told me that she had always felt deep within her heart that she 'knew' things but she lacked the confidence to believe and trust in her insights. She said she had been raised as a Catholic, but had always felt that there was more to religion than she had been taught. She now wanted to reach her higher self. Her second guide, the Egyptian priest, revealed that he had a mission to help Rita reconnect to the part of her soul that stored spiritual and mystical knowledge from the many lifetimes she had spent in Ancient Egypt. She was very excited by this revelation. Rita told me that just a few weeks previously she had joined a religious group based on the teaching and mysticism of Ancient Egypt. She told me how she had always wanted to learn more about the life and spiritual beliefs of Ancient Egypt and was fascinated by what she was currently learning in her group. None of what I relayed to Rita seemed to surprise her as somewhere within her she began to recognise her true self and her feelings of needing more fulfilment in her life. She found a new dimension as she looked forward to discovering more about her higher self.

Tied up with our higher self is our higher purpose. As we progress through the various stages of our earthly existence, from babyhood to childhood, to adolescence and finally to adulthood, we travel from destiny point to destiny point. These destiny points are certain events in our lifetimes on earth that are also events in our spiritual journey. These points are tailored for our highest good, and lead us to accomplish our spiritual reason for being—our higher purpose.

We can choose to take a certain path in life. We can choose a career, a partner, friends, a home, and so on, but if our choice is not in harmony with our spiritual journey, then our guides will steer us towards the path which best suits our higher purpose. This is because our higher purpose is the reason we exist, not just in this life but in all lives and planes.

Finding one's higher purpose in life is not easy. Many people begin their lives on very different pathways from the one which will eventually lead them to discovering, and fulfilling, their higher purpose. Some people may even spend the majority of their earthly lives on a particular path, and when they reach a destiny point their lives change to the path of their spiritual journey. Such was the case with Daphne.

My client, Daphne, had always believed that her true path in life was to be the best wife and mother she could be, and so she had devoted almost all of her adult life to her family. Daphne told me she first became restless when her teenage daughters reached adulthood. Then her daughters left home for university and she felt less and less needed. This thought frightened her, because with no one at home to care for she felt empty and unfulfilled. Her husband, Raymond, was a very busy and successful gynaecologist and didn't need all the care that Daphne had to give. As the years went by, both her daughters developed successful careers, while Daphne felt more and more lost and her health eventually began to deteriorate.

When Daphne came to me for a reading, I didn't see her, psychically, as someone who was moping around the house, wondering where she had made a wrong turn in her life. I saw that she was a nurturer and carer, and that she was also a very intelligent woman with a brilliant mind. During her reading, I told Daphne that I could see her studying at a university in the future. Her spirit guides showed her becoming a doctor. To me, it was just another message from the spirit realm, but Daphne's eyes sparkled and she stared at me with amazement. Apparently, I had hit upon her secret desire—to go to university and to study to become a doctor, just like her husband.

Three years later, I saw Daphne again. As she arrived for her reading, I noticed straightaway that this was a very different person from the one who had been to see me previously. Her health had improved dramatically and she looked ten years younger. She was buoyant and alive. Daphne told me that she was studying medicine and it gave her a joy and purpose she had never experienced before, even though she had been very happy and fulfilled as a wife and mother. She also said that her whole attitude to, and understanding of, life had changed. Apart from thoroughly enjoying her life like never before, she now knew why she had been born. She wanted to help people who were sick.

Daphne is now a well-respected specialist and works with children in a large teaching hospital. She has helped many people. She tells me that at last she felt that she was needed. She says she is grateful that she was challenged to leave the path of her previous existence when her family no longer depended on her, as she is now following her higher purpose in life.

Our higher self is responsible for our spiritual growth so, not surprisingly, it often drives us towards our higher purpose. Most of the time we don't even realise that we are progressing from one destiny point to the next; most of the time we don't know, at first, what propels our actions. Often, the intricate and many strands of our lives seem separate, until we realise our purpose.

Recently, a woman named Merle who lived in the Northern Territory wrote to me asking if she could make two appointments. She felt that I may able to help answer some questions she had been grappling with for quite some time.

Two months later Merle arrived in Sydney to meet me. She was small and her blonde curly hair and blue eyes gave her face a kind and soft look. I was drawn to her immediately. As we began the session, it became obvious that she had a lot to discuss. Merle explained that she had visions of events before these events actually occurred. She told me how she had seen the tsunami in 1998 sweeping across an area of Papua New Guinea and killing many thousands of people before the disaster actually occurred. On another occasion, Merle had a vision of a car bomb in Ireland then she saw it on the television news, exactly as it was in her vision.

Not only were these visions distressing for Merle, particularly as her predictions were so accurate, but she could not understand how or why she was receiving these psychic pictures. Then what, she wondered, was she meant to do with this information, if anything? These questions weighed heavily upon her. She knew, rationally, there was no way that she could intervene and prevent the forthcoming events, but she also felt there must be some reason why she received this information. Led by her instincts, Merle contacted me for help.

As soon as I tuned in, I was told that Merle was in fact an old soul. She had been on earth many times and had acquired a lot of spiritual knowledge both here and in other planes of existence. She had therefore come into this life with fairly advanced gifts of clairvoyance and clairaudience.

I was told that Merle was to be a teacher in this lifetime, and that her purpose now was to train others to be aware of nature's gifts and to honour them. I could also see Merle working with children and that she would ultimately develop special nature programs for schools that would then be implemented on a broad scale. As I saw it, her task in this lifetime was to link children with nature.

Merle was delighted with this message. She informed me that she was studying a course in social ecology at university and that she could now see the link between this and her higher purpose.

I also saw that Merle had been given the gift of writing as well as the gift of insight. I told her how I could see her channelling her intuitive gifts into writing, and the she would write children's books that encouraged children to connect with nature. I knew she would have a great career in writing.

Now Merle was really astounded. She told me that she had already begun to write, but no one else knew. 'Sometimes,' she said, 'the urge is so strong, I get all this information in my head and I just have to write it down, even if it is in the middle of the night.'

Merle certainly had a very highly developed sense of intuition. Her psychic gifts, her insights, her path of study and her need to write all linked to her higher purpose. In that reading all I really did was encourage Merle to follow her intuition and show her that she already had all of the pieces for her future life. All she had to do was put these pieces together and then build a rewarding life for herself from her gifts and talents.

Merle's story shows how important it is for each and every one of us to listen to our intuition, and allow it to guide us throughout our lives on earth, for it will lead to our higher purpose. Merle, you and I—everyone—to some degree or another, built up knowledge throughout many lifetimes, and even in between lifetimes on other planes. This stored knowledge is available to you always, if you trust yourself and your intuition.

We all have gut feelings or a 'sixth sense'. We get inklings about certain situations or people, but usually our head takes over and our rational thinking overrides our insight, and immediately the connection with our inner wisdom is gone.

However, when we learn to use our intuition and trust our instincts, we see life more clearly. We become more and more aware of truth, and we begin to know, without a shadow of a doubt, whether or not something is right for us. This is because our intuition comes directly from our higher selves.

If you have not yet found your higher purpose, then I urge you to be open to discovering this for yourself. Listen to your heart and don't be frightened to follow your instincts, for they will lead you to the real reason for your existence—fulfilling your higher purpose. We all have insight and awareness, we all are given glimpses of what lies ahead for us. We just need to be brave enough to recognise what we really want to do with our lives and then go ahead and do it.

So we've talked about our higher self, but how do we find it? There are many ways of tapping into our higher self. One is by meditating, which helps us let go of the conscious mind. We become more peaceful and more in control of our thoughts and feelings, and eventually we will be more able to tap into our higher consciousness to find answers to our questions. When we connect with our higher selves in this way, we will be able to understand ourselves better and make the correct decisions and choices.

To tap into your higher self through meditation, try the following exercise.

Sit alone in a quiet place where you will not be disturbed. Make yourself comfortable and make sure that there is total peace and quiet. Have a pen and paper handy. In this exercise, you will be endeavouring to reach answers given from your higher self. Now ask yourself the question, 'What in my life do I want to change?' Close your eyes and listen to your mind. Allow yourself to flow with the thoughts and images that you may experience. If you find that your mind is blank, that's quite all right. Don't panic. Simply keep on trying. Patience and persistence may be required for success.

Next, open your eyes and take a deep breath and relax. Now, try again. This time you may progress. Follow your thoughts and images and listen for answers. If you still don't succeed, keep trying. Eventually you will succeed.

You will know when you have connected with your higher self because you will have a decisive and positive feeling about the answer to your question—you will 'know' with certainty that the answer is correct, just like you know your own name.

Write down the answers you receive from your meditation. You have now taken a major step towards creating a better life for yourself and towards fulfilling your higher purpose.

Another simple exercise to establish a connection with your higher self is to simply ask for the answer to your problem. All you need to do is find a quiet moment then ask the question to your higher self. This technique works best when the questions are simple and direct, such as those that can be answered yes or no.

Make the question specific and ask the question clearly.

Listen to your inner voice for the answer.

Your first response to the question will come from instinct and your higher self.

If you hear nothing, wait and the answer might come to you by another means. Perhaps someone will say something later, or you might read a book with the answer in it or hear the answer in a song. Remember to be patient. You will know the answer when you get the feeling of certainty.

We should always examine ourselves to ensure we are making decisions from our higher self, and not our lower self. Over time, we should aim to raise our levels of understanding so that we will operate automatically from our higher selves. If we allow our lower selves to take over, we can lose touch with the real purpose of life. It is easy to become entrenched with the problems of everyday life and become blinded to the truth of our being. Once we recognise that everything in life belongs to a higher order, we can put our problems into perspective, as opportunities to learn on our journey to spiritual fulfilment.

While you should allow your higher self to direct your life, it is important to remember that it is your life and no one else can live it for you. If you want changes in your life, you must make them.

Never allow fear of change to stop you from moving forward in your life. It is very normal to be afraid of change—most of us are. However, if we go forward in spite of our fear, then we will discover that the fear we had will lose its intensity as we progress. And as we achieve more of what we want, we will fear less and less. Once you have decided which changes you want to make in your life, then go ahead and make them. Be brave. If you listen to your higher self, you *will* move forward in your journey, and you need never look back.

We are more than we know. Every soul is a complex, amazing, astounding energy and there is so much more to us than who we are in this lifetime. Even if we spent every waking hour of this lifetime trying, we could never imagine the whole magnificence of ourselves. What a wonder we are.

Each of us has been given the gift of a higher self. This is the part of ourselves which knows who we really are and what is really best for us to achieve the highest potential in all aspects of life. The higher self is always available to us to tap into and to give us the answers we seek to decisions we must make. Access to the higher self is best achieved by meditation. If you can let all your worries and thoughts go and find that place of inner peace then you are clear and free to find the answers from your higher self. Always remember that patience is the key to accessing your higher self. Patience and persistence will lead you there. Meditate and ask for direction for your life and before long you will have your answers.

Linda's session has stayed with me for a long time, because it reinforced many of the concepts I had held about the way in which the universe rewards us for our strength and patience. Linda had these two gifts in abundance.

Linda was a lovely lady with a delicate quality about her. After we had settled down for the session I began to tune in to Linda's guides to see what messages I might receive about her relationship and her career.

The first message I picked up was that Linda was struggling with life. In fact, every area of her life was a struggle. Linda was a herbalist. She had opened her own business and had been operating a shop in a busy part of the city for the past five years. She was clearly a hard worker and had a lot of strength, but it was a difficult business for her since several other herbalists had come to her part of town. They too had opened up shops in which they both consulted and sold their herbs. However, as Linda was the first one to choose that particular location, and she had signed a long lease, she was determined not to let competition stop her from succeeding. She was also raising her ten-year-old daughter whom she loved very much. Life was tough, but always she had found the strength to get her through.

I saw that in about a year's time she would find her business life easier, and that a partner would come into her life. He would work alongside her and share the cost of her rent and her overheads. When I described this man to her Linda smiled. She recognised the person I was describing. They had met at a course recently and she was delighted at the thought that they could be working together in the future.

We then moved on to look at what was happening in Linda's relationships. Immediately, I saw a man in her life who was causing her a lot of difficulty. This was the part of her where she longed most for peace and happiness. The man I saw was older and it appeared that he was stuck in his own life. He wanted to be in Linda's life, but only on his terms, and while he was happy to see her once or twice a week as he had been doing for some three years he was not prepared to make any kind of commitment to her or to their relationship. Basically, he was in complete control of the relationship. Linda said she was unhappy about the situation, but she admitted that she felt trapped in the relationship because she loved him and did not want to lose him. The thought of being without his friendship scared her and so she settled for less than she truly deserved.

Interestingly, the universe has ways of balancing out unfair situations, and as I peered into Linda's future I saw that the universe was about to spring into action and set things right. I saw Linda meeting another man in the not-too-distant future. He was young, attractive and vibrant, and he too was a healer. I saw that he would be kind to her and love her very much.

I told her that she would have a major decision to make about which partner she would choose to be with, that her current friend, Tom, would certainly have to shape up or ship out and that the competition between the two men would be quite intense.

Linda knew her relationship with Tom was stagnant and she wanted to release herself from it, but she found it hard to do so because she loved him. Knowing that a new man would soon be in her life, Linda brightened up. She was thrilled to think that she was important enough for the universe to give her a choice of relationships. She knew immediately that she'd prefer to have a fresh start with someone new, with someone who got on with the relationship.

Once Linda's session was finished she told me how pleased she felt. She knew that her life would go on even after she had ended her current non-progressive relationship. 'The universe will always step in to bring universal justice where required. And remember, you are never alone. Your guides do look after you,' I assured her. As Linda waved goodbye she said that when the time came I would be invited to her wedding so I could see the man I had described to her in the flesh. I smiled as I visualised that happy day.

What a wonderful comfort it is to know that we are protected and given what we deserve if we honour ourselves and our universe. Linda's guides were obviously ready to help her make great changes in her life. I am now happy to report that Linda is planning her wedding with the new man in her life. She was bubbling with excitement when she phoned me a year after her session to tell me how delighted she is with her new life.

7

Finding our way through difficult times and relationships

Sometimes in life when we are going through a difficult or particularly challenging experience, we tend to feel that we are being dealt an unfair blow that we just can't cope with. But I believe that we have been born armed to fight and win any battle we might encounter here on earth. The older we are in a soul sense, the more challenges we are likely to encounter during our lifetime. And the older we are as a soul, the more able we are to deal with life, because we are more aware of our resources. I believe we are never required to face situations in life that we cannot manage, because the universe is here to help us to embrace our own magnificence, not to punish us. This is a spiritual truth.

Another spiritual truth is that we have free will and can choose to do what we will with our lives. This means that we can choose to stand up to our troubles or we can choose to escape from them and run away. What we do is our choice. If we decide to not face troubles or spiritual tests in this lifetime, they will return to us again and again until we have been able to successfully deal with them. This happens because our soul is constantly growing and moving to new levels of awareness and life situations, in order to progress through eternity.

I believe that we are given a particular test three times in life, and if we fail that test three times we will have to deal with the same spiritual test in another lifetime. That's why it is easier and better for the soul to face and pass the test in this lifetime. If we bear in mind that we can succeed, because we are fully equipped, then we will have less apprehension when attempting to deal with the problems we face. Both happy and difficult times lie before us, but we are equipped to pass the tests and to keep on progressing. Our soul will be filled with wisdom and we will carry this truth with us throughout our entire existence. The more we grow spiritually, the more we know spiritually. In this sense, the universe takes its cue from us; we actually direct what happens to us to draw to us those lessons our soul needs.

There is unlimited joy in succeeding over difficulties. It feels great when you have undergone a huge battle in life and *won*. If you have ever been sick and your doctor tells you that you are now one hundred per cent well again, don't you feel fantastic? The same feeling comes to us in many other situations in which we are victorious. These triumphs are given to us to balance our lives.

In nature and in life there is always balance. Just think about the seasons—the cold weather is eventually replaced by the hot weather, the rain by the sun, and so it goes. Balance and harmony bring joy and restoration to life. Suffering is replaced by happiness and the cycle continues.

Perspective is the key to coping with the different stages in life. Putting things into perspective allows us to alleviate much of our suffering and replace it with joy, because even in the most painful event in life, there is some joy around us. Finding our way through pain or sorrow isn't easy. We need to draw upon inner strength that we have not ever used before. We also need to call on all our resources and be in tune with our guides, our higher self and God. But we can do this because God never gives us a situation that He does not equip us to handle. If we don't use our strengths we don't actually lose them, but we may eventually lose our ability to access them with ease.

It does help if we can remember that however hard the situation, ultimately it is temporary. Time really is a great healer. As time passes, situations change and our pain will be less in a few years' or months' time. This is because nothing in the universe remains still. We are here on a vast continuum and time is constantly pushing us forward.

Like perspective, our attitude plays a huge role in how we manage to deal with suffering. If, instead of seeing ourselves as victims, we look for the lessons in each moment, we can start to benefit from the experience. Often we agonise over situations that never eventuate and we end up worrying needlessly.

Each one of us has to decide what we want in life. It takes determination and clear focus to do this, and then courage, patience and strength to wait for it to be delivered to us. This also involves faith and trust, because we have no real guarantee, in an earthly sense, that we will receive what we want. However, there is such a thing as universal justice. No trust that we have in the universe will ever be unreciprocated. The universe gives rewards where they are warranted.

We also need to learn patience and tolerance because they enhance our strength and courage, and help us remain focused on our goals and dreams. If we remain centred and strong, we will attain our dreams, even though the exact details may be changed by the greater wisdom of the universe. In the end, the universe knows far better what is right for us and when the right time is to deliver it to us.

Sometimes, though, we can feel as if we're having to use all of our strengths and our spiritual gifts while we wait patiently for the universe to bring what we want. But we can rest assured that if we do wait and if we pass the tests of patience, tolerance, courage, strength, determination and focus, our dream will be delivered to us and the rewards will be endless.

At times in life we can feel like we have hit a wall. Many people complain to me that they feel as if they have been pushed into a corner with no where to go and quite often no one to turn to for help. This is a dark place to find yourself in, full of confusion and depression, and it can make life seem almost unbearable.

During this phase of a journey, we need to reach out for help to find that inner strength which we all have and which will be the lifeline to hold on to while we work to free ourselves and regain our feelings of purpose and motivation.

If no help is available then we must help ourselves. One way of achieving this is to turn inwards and find our higher self. The higher self will reconnect us to the best part of life, and within it is wisdom, comfort and purpose. Our higher self has the correct answers about the right direction for us.

When we access our higher self, we will discover that our attitudes will change—and we will let go of feelings of defeat and instead become victors in our own lives. This will help us experience a renewed sense of self and a recognition of the true purpose of our existence. It's good to feel like you have a plan of action to call upon in times of distress. Taking action is the first step in turning the situation around.

Sometimes we can surprise ourselves by our actions and discover some hidden strengths. Whenever this topic comes up, I think about Raelene, a woman who exemplifies the ability to tap into her inner strengths.

When I first met Raelene, she was divorced and was determined never to allow herself to be a victim of life. She had spent much of her life as a nurse and her career was important to her. She was a very strong person and was living alone, which is exactly how she wanted it to be at that time.

At her first session with me I saw that Raelene was soon to meet a new man. He was tall and good looking with a beard. I described him and told Raelene that she would soon be a happier woman because they would become very close. Raelene was pleased with this news.

A couple of weeks after this session Raelene phoned me to tell me she had met a man, Craig, and she was thrilled as he had asked her out to dinner.

A few months later Raelene telephoned me again. This time she wanted to make an appointment for a session for herself and for Craig. On the appointed day I opened my door to see Raelene standing on the front porch holding the arm of man who looked exactly as I had seen psychically, and so I felt as if we had already met and that I knew him quite well. When I tuned in, I told them both that I could see a happy relationship ahead with each other. They certainly seemed to be in love, and as I waved them goodbye at the end I saw them walking down the path arm in arm.

A little while later Raelene and Craig got married. I saw them once or twice a year for the next ten years and their happiness seemed endless. Then one day my phone rang and a very solemn Raelene asked if she could book an appointment.

When Raelene came for her session it was obvious that she had been crying. 'It's Craig,' she sobbed, wiping her eyes with a tissue. 'He's met another woman and I know her quite well. It's so cruel because they've been seeing each other for six months or so and I never knew.' She was devastated and wanted to know why I didn't tell her this would happen. My answer was that I didn't actually see it.

Raelene wanted answers. As we looked at the issues in her current life situation I felt satisfied that Raelene's strength would return when she'd had time to process this situation. Raelene had the choice of staying in her marriage or taking the hard road to dissolving it. I did not envy her—making a decision to leave a marriage is never easy.

Months passed by and soon it was Christmas time. I usually received a Christmas card from Raelene and this year was no exception. She sent a lovely card to me with warm wishes and greetings from the Bahamas. Raelene had decided to not suffer from her situation. She informed me in the accompanying letter that she had told Craig to leave, which he had done, and she and a girlfriend of many years were now celebrating her freedom in the Bahamas.

A few months later, I heard that Craig and his new friend were living together, but that Raelene had also found a new man in her life and she was living with him. I was pleased that Raelene was not suffering and was delighted some months later when an invitation arrived in the mail inviting me to her wedding. This was a happy ending for someone who could have felt bitter and victimised, but who used her strength and willpower to rise above her obstacles to find joy and happiness with a new man who truly valued her.

When I reflect on this situation I believe that I am not allowed to see a relationship ending before it really begins. If I told people this they may find the whole idea of entering upon a relationship that is doomed too daunting to undertake. Relationships are given to us for many reasons, not the least of which is to help us grow and to become more aware spiritually. When we stop growing and can't gain any more spiritual awareness from that relationship it will end and we then move on to a new learning situation in our lives.

I am only allowed to 'see' and deliver what is in the best interest for the person for their highest growth, and I really don't see *all* the details and difficulties that people will face on their journey through life.

As humans we are often vulnerable to our emotions. Our feelings can override our better judgment if we are not fully aware of what is causing us to make decisions and to act in particular ways. So we must learn to balance our thoughts with our emotions and to make decisions that are best for our growth in every way.

Relationships are one of the greatest arenas for learning how to balance our lives and to make the right choices. Finding our way through the sometimes difficult realm of relationship issues can be confusing as well as rewarding. This was true for Evonne.

Evonne was in her mid-fifties when she came to see me. She had married quite young and she and her husband David had a lovely son called Peter. David worked as a coal miner and Evonne stayed home to take care of her son. She was a good wife and mother, and their small family was very happy. Peter grew to be a strong and happy teenager. Then one day a dreadful event occurred that shattered their lives. David was working in the mine when, without warning, it collapsed and many of the miners were killed.

David managed to escape, but not without serious injury. He was hit by flying debris and suffered severe brain damage. David recovered physically, but it soon became clear that the brain damage had affected his emotions, causing him to lose all sense of feelings.

Naturally, this changed his character and he became increasingly more difficult to deal with. Even though Peter and Evonne loved David, they found it impossible to live with him. Eventually, Peter left home and moved into a flat with a couple of his mates. Evonne agonised over his leaving, but things went well for Peter. He managed to find a job in the motor industry and found a joy and relief that he had not experienced since his dad's accident.

Evonne also found a job that she enjoyed and made many new friends, and David began to adjust to his injuries and was able to look after himself quite well. Life continued on for all three for some time, but eventually the strain of living with a man who had no emotions became too heavy for Evonne to bear so she decided to move to a flat close by. She worked hard and kept on visiting her husband to make sure he was managing. To her relief and joy she found that David was doing really well. A few years later, Evonne met another man with whom she fell in love. He was kind and caring, and Evonne was beginning to feel safe and happy with her new partner, Brian.

By this stage, much of the trauma surrounding the accident had gone and Evonne was relatively relaxed and happy, except that by nature she was a worrier. Even though she had no need to, she still agonised over the wellbeing of her son and husband.

Things were going really well with Brian until one day he announced that he had to go to another city to see his ex-wife and children. Evonne was terrified that Brian might end up staying there and reunite with his wife and family. She became increasingly anxious and before long all the old patterns of worry returned. She couldn't eat or sleep while Brian was away and, even though he telephoned her every day, she still agonised over his leaving. She came to see me because she was suffering so much that she had made herself quite ill.

When I tuned in for her I could see that Brian had to finish off business matters with his ex-wife and that the marriage was truly over. Brian loved his children and even though they were now grown up, he took the opportunity to visit them and renew the bonds between them. I could also see that he did love Evonne and that he would return to her in the near future.

As I told her this I could see her relaxing. I assured her that she and Brian would make a happy life together. I also saw her son Peter being very successful in business and I told her that he was going to buy his own business and that it would do very well. I could also see that David was quite contented and doing well.

I assured Evonne that her life would work out well for her. I then told her that her responsibility was to herself and that she was to stop worrying and start to eat and sleep again. Evonne needed to learn to put her concerns into perspective and to try to find a balance in her life. By tuning in to her guides, I was able to give her the assurance she needed to encourage her to hold on to her positive energy so that she could continue to move forward in her life journey, and not become paralysed with fear and negativity.

The mind is truly amazing. With your mind you can control every aspect of your life, and make dreams come true. Even though it may sometimes be hard to grasp this truth, your reality is what your mind manifests. Most of us are unaware of the power, strength and ability of our own minds.

By thinking with and focusing on positive energy, I believe anything is possible. In the case of Evonne, focusing on positive energy helped her to stop fear and negativity from taking over her life. We can do this by tapping into our subconscious, which helps us connect with our higher self and our guides.

I have often seen people with life-threatening illnesses use the power of their subconscious to overcome illness. Every day we use our subconscious minds to manifest into our lives those things—people, places, events, experiences—that we need or desire. Our subconscious mind feeds the conscious mind. So if we have the right attitudes at the subconscious level then we will automatically program our conscious mind to work in the same way. This is why affirmations are so powerful and can change a person's life. One of the most powerful affirmations is one discovered by a great healer who lived a long time ago. His name was Emile Coue and he was amongst the first great minds to use hypnosis.

Every day in every way I am getting better and better is a powerful tool to use to program the subconscious mind. If this is repeated out loud and silently often enough, then the one saying it soon begins to change their state of being for the better.

Hypnotherapists use the power of affirmations by placing their patients into a state of relaxation where the conscious mind is distracted and positive thoughts and suggestions are fed to the subconscious mind. Many people are able to overcome all kinds of problems using hypnosis as a tool. We can also program our subconscious through meditation.

Relationships can be exhilarating as well as painful and we all will experience the highs and lows of relationship issues during our lives. There has to be a very good reason why we go through all the troubles that we do. If we keep in mind that all of the issues and hurts have been given to us to learn from and to grow spiritually then we will accept the situation better and be better able to find the resources to enable us to deal with the situation and move forward in our lives.

When life is hard it helps to remember that we are never alone. We have angels to protect and watch over us. So if ever we feel abandoned we need to reach out and ask our angels for help.

Along with this help, we must use our inner resources to strengthen us and to get us through. Cindy-Lou is a woman with endless strength and an ability to *use* that strength. Her courage is truly inspiring and her strength undeniable.

When Cindy-Lou came to see me for a reading I sensed her loneliness and suffering. 'You are alone in life,' I said. 'Yes, I am—and how did you know?' 'Well,' I laughed, 'I am psychic and you are here for a reading.' With that, Cindy-Lou laughed too and readied herself for her session.

Looking into Cindy-Lou's soul was a rewarding experience. I could see that this lady was truly incredible. I saw that her husband had left her and that for more than a year Cindy-Lou had been sad and alone. She had three children to raise and the eldest one, a boy, was just ten years old.

Cindy-Lou had courage and strength, and these virtues shone brightly from within her soul. Her strength had carried her through the difficulties of the past twelve months, and her love for her children, coupled with her determination to be the best parent in the world, gave her the will to survive.

I was able to encourage and praise her for her strengths. I could see that there were many times in the past year that Cindy-Lou had felt lost, confused and abandoned. She found it difficult to comprehend that her husband, who had been so loyal and kind to her and the children, would suddenly become so cruel towards her and the children before he left.

It was all so unexpected and I could see that she was suffering from shock. I could see, too, her wonderful commitment to herself and her family, and I knew that she would be rewarded: her strength would not fail her. She was surprised by her own strength and she admitted that she was pleased with herself that she had not given in to weakness and fear.

When I looked into Cindy-Lou's future I saw happiness ahead. She and the children would be moving from the current home. She had been concerned as to whether this move would be the best thing for her children, but I assured her that a move would bring new energy and usher a new beginning to take her to the next stage of her life. I also told her that the children will be delighted.

I saw a new love in her life, too. This man was kind and caring and was genuine in his feelings and attitude towards her and the children. Cindy-Lou had already met him, but was taking the relationship slowly, so as not to be disillusioned and let down. She was also very conscious of protecting her children from any further trauma—they had suffered enough by their father's departure.

As I looked further into the future, I saw her ex-husband begging her forgiveness and wanting to be accepted back into the family. Cindy-Lou had a mixed reaction to this news. Part of her was happy, but another part was cautious.

I could see that she would have a choice between the two men in her life and that choice would be hers alone to make. I did not tell her what I saw about her choice, because she needed to be able to choose her future without prejudice.

Cindy-Lou would study in the near future. That was clear to see. She squealed with excitement when I told her so, and she agreed that she truly hoped to study and ensure a well-paid career for herself. I saw success in this endeavour, and she immediately decided to seek out an application form for the course she had wanted to undertake for such a long time.

Cindy-Lou was beginning to brighten up. She told me how much better she felt, as she could see that her strength would see her through, and that her life would become easier and more rewarding in the very near future. When she left my home, I felt truly pleased that I had been fortunate enough to glimpse into the life of a truly strong and wonderful woman, knowing that her courage and strength would be applauded by the universe.

It is never easy to extract ourselves from relationships in a compassionate way. When the time comes to move on and leave behind someone we have loved or still do love, we have to muster up enormous strength and courage. No matter how unhappy we may have felt within the relationship, we must show compassion and understanding for the partner we are leaving behind. Remember, if we find ourselves in this situation, that person we are now leaving is someone we once loved very deeply.

Life has moved us on. Growth and sometimes even the universe has moved us on. It's not anybody's fault. We cannot lay blame upon our partner or ourselves. As long as we have tried our best and been kind and caring towards our partner, we can move ahead with our life with a deep sense of inner peace that we have done the very best that we could. We will then have no guilt. And even in our thoughts it is good to send our partner love and protective energy so that our higher self reaches their higher self, and peace and harmony will always be between us, both in this world and the next. Be compassionate and you will receive compassion in return.

Bill's story illustrates exactly this point. He had been in a relationship with Sue. They had been together unhappily for more than ten years. Both of them came to see me for separate readings and they'd decided to stay together even though life continued to be difficult for them both.

Once I tuned in for Bill I realised that his world was indeed unsettled. He had fallen in love with another woman, but even though he was enjoying the benefits of a new relationship it too was fraught with problems. I could see that Bill would need enormous strength if he was to find the happiness which had eluded him for most of his adult life because, basically, he was in no-man's land.

I was able to explain to him that he was holding on to his past whilst at the same time trying to reach out to his future. When we do this the universe receives very mixed messages, and as a result it cannot assist us. The simple fact is that if we want something new, then we need to let go of the old.

Of course, one of the most basic needs we have is for security. This is, of course, quite normal whether it be a yearning for physical security or psychological security. The universe however, will not allow us to hold onto everything that we think we need for our security, because at some point in our evolution we reach the stage where our faith is tested.

There is a wonderful saying: if we jump the net appears. Sometimes we need to let go of the past and have faith that we will be looked after. If Bill was to find true happiness he needed to make some major decisions, then act on them. In his case he was still living with Sue, but loving Ella. This position was further complicated by the fact that Ella was from a completely different cultural and religious background. She had only emigrated to Australia eight years previously and because of the strict practices of her culture, she had not been allowed to mix with men who weren't from her own country and culture. So here was Bill in love with a woman who he could not easily win, and who would have to overcome enormous obstacles within her own life in order to be with him. What was he to do?

As I tried to gain guidance for Bill's problems, the spiritual lessons became abundantly clear. First, Bill had to make up his mind whether he wanted to be with Sue or Ella. When it came down to it there was absolutely no choice for Bill, because Ella was the woman he loved and wanted to be with. That settled, Bill then needed to find the courage to say goodbye to Sue, then separate completely from her.

I explained to him that the universe would help him make this happen more easily once he gave out a clear message that this was what he wanted. By this stage the weight on

Bill's shoulders was beginning to ease as he realised that the impossible situation was going to be removed.

His next problem was Ella's cultural background. Bill and I explored some of the issues that couples need to face when their ethnic backgrounds differ. Bill was adamant that he loved Ella so much that he would accept and welcome the differences between them. He assured me he was prepared to work to embrace all issues required of him. He believed that he could happily hand over his future children to his in-laws for education in their ways and he saw this opportunity as one of expansion for his future offspring.

I reminded him that this may be easier to say than to do, but Bill felt strongly on the matter. I could see that he had the strength and determination needed to assist him in the future. This covered, I then ventured further into what lay ahead for him. I could see him standing beside Ella, and the bond between them growing with each obstacle placed in their way. I told him that I knew that they could be happy together if he had enough willpower, courage and determination to fight each battle as it came along. I could also see that Ella truly loved Bill and that in some way Bill was the catalyst to releasing her from the bonds of her past. They could be very happy, but there were many hurdles to face before they would be able to build a life together.

Bill gained a lot of strength from the knowledge that he had enough inner fortitude and love, and that Ella also had enough inner strength and love for them to combine forces and overcome all obstacles to their being together. He recommitted to the battle ahead with a firm determination to stay focused on his future and centred within himself. He knew that the next year would not be easy. He also knew that if he persisted he could find true happiness, as long as he was prepared to sacrifice some of his old familiar life for his new one.

As we finished the session, Bill announced that he might be needing to visit me more often in the future to help him overcome his forthcoming hurdles. I smiled and told him that he was welcome to see me again, but that really he was well equipped with spiritual tools for earthly battles as long as he did not lose sight of his goals.

In moving on with his own life and allowing his love to be directed towards someone who was happy to receive it and who was able to give love in return, Bill was releasing himself from the negative, unhappy energy he had been sharing for so long with Sue. By moving out of his relationship with Sue, he was diminishing the negative energy he was giving to Sue, and which she was giving him in return. This would release both of them to their best futures.

It is rewarding to see people managing their lives and, in particular, their relationship issues with confidence and determination. Such was the case with Stacey.

Stacey came to see me because she wanted to know about her life in general and, in particular, about her relationships and work life. When I tuned in I found that Stacey was enjoying a very balanced existence and that she had been in this space for some time. I also saw that she was looking for a partner who was neither possessive nor dependent. Stacey agreed that she was waiting for the right man to come along.

As we progressed with the session I found that Stacey had been bitterly disappointed by men in the past and that even though she was at times lonely, she was not prepared to settle for less than what she was looking for. Stacey agreed that it was hard going certainly, but she also told me that she had found a wonderful peace and contentment living an independent life.

I did see her with a wonderful man in the future. They were holding hands and travelling together along the same path. They were very much in love. The man concerned was clever, and had devoted his working life to helping underprivileged people. He travelled a great deal with his work and he was quite developed spiritually.

Stacey's eyes widened as I described the future to her. She confided that she had always dreamed she could help people who were suffering. She was delighted when I told her that her man had musical talents and that he was a Buddhist. She smiled as she told me that she too enjoyed the Buddhist teachings and had been an active member of a Buddhist group for some years. Even though Stacey was happy, she had longed for a companion.

Then as we talked on about her work, I was suddenly told by Stacey's guide that her man was American and that Stacey would spend many years in the United States. She laughed as she explained to me that she loved America. She had visited the country often and every time she had been there she wished that she could live there. Having thanked me, Stacey left the session feeling very positive about her future. She was determined to continue along her path until the time came for her to meet her partner.

I do love to see a client who displays courage, strength and determination to accept in life only the very best, and right situation, for herself. In Stacey's case, she would be very happily rewarded for her strengths and determination. You see, universal plans are always so perfect for us. If we interfere with them either by being too pushy or rushing in and settling for less than what is right, then the universe loses the opportunity to deliver the very best plans for us.

When Stacey decided to wait for her life to open up, bringing opportunities to her, she was allowing the universe to bring her a life situation which was perfect for her mind, body and spirit. All areas of her being would be catered for in a truly wonderful way. Stacey had made the right decision, as her life in the future was to show.

After she left I thought how wonderful it was that the universe rewards us for our patience and for not accepting less than we truly want. I admired Stacey for her strength and I was delighted to see that she would soon find what she was hoping for. This confirmed my belief that the universe knows best what is right for us and, if we wait, the universe will deliver.

Sometimes we have to wait for what we want because the universe has a perfect time plan for us. Our own impatience can often mislead us into thinking that we are ready for some situation in life when in fact we are not. There are many reasons why we may not be ready.

About a year later, I heard from Stacey. She was bubbling with excitement as she revealed to me that she had found the man that we had discussed during her session with me. He was all that Stacey had dreamed of and they were now happily planning their future together.

Once again, I was delighted that the universe had delivered what it promises to those who have the courage and determination to use their spiritual strengths and work in harmony with the universe.

Too often we spend our lives dreaming of all the things we'd like to have. If only we were able to do this or acquire that, then we're convinced that magically life will be happy for us. However, we need to be mindful of everything we seek because sometimes those things that appear the most tantalising can end up being quite the opposite for us.

Let me tell you about Martha, a woman in her mid-fifties, who came to see me for a reading. Martha was a very stylish woman who appeared to be very capable and confident. When she arrived at my door one cold and windy day I could tell that she was a little uneasy about the session.

As she settled into the chair Martha explained that she had only ever had one reading previously. That session was some eleven years ago and upon reflection she had been amazed by the accuracy of the predictions. Her life had travelled along the path that had been predicted and so now she felt that she was at crossroads and was unsure of the direction she should take.

My first psychic impression of Martha's current life was that she was lonely and unhappy. I could tell that she had been struggling with many problems and that she had become totally confused about which decisions to make. I saw that her husband, who was younger than she, was involved with another woman, who was very young. As Martha's husband was in his mid-forties, this meant quite an age difference in the lives of the lovers.

Martha began to cry as I unveiled her present situation. 'You know,' she said, 'what makes the whole thing so dreadful is that I actually prayed that Bob would meet another woman and that he would leave me for her, but now that he has actually found someone else and my prayers have been answered my life is in a dreadful mess.'

Her husband Bob and his girlfriend Mandy had been thrown together through Bob's work and they were seeing each other every day as they worked in close proximity. Martha was distraught. She was angry at herself for wanting to get out of her marriage in the beginning but now, once threatened with the prospect of losing her marriage, she no longer wanted to see her husband move on. She was also angry with herself for not having the courage and strength to change her current circumstances—to demand that her husband leave or end his other relationship.

Martha assured me that if she did not have an eight-year-old daughter there would be no question about forcing her husband to leave.

The affair had been going on for six months and Martha had lost a lot of self-esteem. She was amazed that even though she could see her situation so clearly she was unable to do something about it. I encouraged her to try to see her situation objectively, as if this was happening to someone else, and then think about what she would advise the person to do in that situation.

It was unacceptable for her to stay in the marriage when her husband had a girlfriend, and so finally she determined to gather up her strength and take action to get a better deal for herself and her daughter. Martha blamed herself for praying that Bob meet someone else, but I told her that it isn't quite as simple as that. It is important to be careful what we ask for because the universe might just deliver and then we have to bear the consequences. But ultimately, we are responsible for our actions and how we treat the people around us, and Bob needed to bear the responsibility for his treatment of Martha.

Martha decided that she would talk to Bob and ask him to move out of home to give her and her daughter a break, and to give him the space to make up his mind about what he really wanted. When Martha left, she felt relieved that at last she had made a decision to take a step to change her life for the better.

The universe had really demonstrated its enormous power and strength. It had shown Martha very clearly and pointedly that it *will* react to any genuine request. Any act within the world generates a reaction at the universal level. Martha had a direct demonstration of this truth. When she asked the universe to allow Bob to meet another woman, because she was unhappy in her marriage, the universe took her request at face value. I truly believe that Martha was only half-hearted in her request, but the universe heard her and acted on what it heard.

Martha's story shows us that we need to ask the universe for things that we really want, things that we believe will help us to improve our life or assist us in making good decisions. This requires us to really tune in to our higher self and examine what it is that we are searching for, and what would fulfill our heart's desires.

Relationships are given to us from the spiritual realm for us to learn spiritual lessons for our growth. They are a rich source of spiritual energy and if we can view them from this perspective we will benefit greatly. Negative energy breeds negativity while positive energy breeds positivity. If we are feeling unhappy then we will subconsciously transfer negative feelings towards our partner. If we are feeling lost and unsettled and unable to give of our very best to our partner, then we need to take responsibility for recognising that we are feeding negative energy to our partner. If we surround someone with negative energy, then we can only expect to receive negative energy. If we know that we are stuck and cannot move beyond our own negativity, we not only owe it to ourselves, but we also owe it to our partner to do something to change this energy.

We could talk to our partner and ask for their advice, go to a counsellor or visit a friend. If all the options we choose fail, then in order not to stop our partner's progress and growth and happiness, we might need to separate and release them, and ourselves, from the negative energy of the relationship.

If we fail to resolve all of the issues which have caused problems for us and then move on to the next relationship, we will simply carry all of the unresolved issues with us into the next relationship. And so this will simply add to our frustration and unhappiness, causing our new partner to suffer. This is a spiritual fact: what we put out is what we get back.

When Leona came to see me, she was in her late twenties. I could see that she was fairly relaxed about the reading. After an initial chat I learned that this was her very first psychic session.

Leona asked me to tune in to the usual areas that people like guidance with—health, relationships and career. It was easy for me to see what was happening. I told her that I could see that she was having severe doubts about remaining in her relationship. Her partner was often quite moody and had a very strong personality. Leona nodded in agreement. Then as I tuned in more deeply I could see that Leona's partner was an older woman.

The couple were very committed to each other. They shared a small house in the city and had made plans to stay together for the rest of their lives. Yet in spite of all this life had become quite difficult for Leona. Increasingly, she was feeling lost in the relationship as her own needs were being neglected. She had always tried to please her partner at the expense of fulfilling her own wishes.

I explained to Leona what happens spiritually when we allow someone else to dominate us. I told her that she was opting out of her responsibility to herself. When this happens we can only find trouble ahead for ourselves.

Leona's guides told her about the need to draw strong boundaries around herself, and to communicate her needs to her partner. After all, how could she expect Sara, her partner, to know what she wanted in life if she didn't articulate this to her? Leona smiled as she began to see the truth clearly.

As she related more and more to what her guides were telling her I could see that already changes were being made in her thinking. She realised that Sara treated her only in the manner which she, Leona, had allowed. She had put up with unfair treatment by not stating clearly that she wanted to be treated differently.

Having satisfied this area of imbalance we then proceeded to investigate Leona's future. I was able to see that provided she worked carefully on the relationship, she could well be with Sara for many years to come. This pleased Leona as she had always hoped that she would grow old with Sara.

I could also see a career move for Leona. I knew that she would change jobs in about twelve months' time and that the career change would involve some study. The next area that I tuned in to was her health. I was not surprised to find that Leona was suffering from stress-related illnesses, because I could see that Leona's physical body was showing somewhat red and raw-looking nerve-endings. Her organs also looked distressed.

What I was seeing was a vision of internal nerves, tissues and organs. If you have ever seen an X-ray then you will know how the picture appears black and white with shading of light and dark areas. That is how I see into a physical body when I am taking a psychic look at someone's health.

'It's no use bottling up your anger and thoughts,' I told her. 'You need to express what is troubling you and discuss whatever you are concerned about to the relevant people, no matter who they are.' Leona knew that stress had in fact been the cause of her severe headaches and backaches. She asked me to help her by suggesting herbal remedies which would calm her. This I did gladly.

As wonderful as relationships can be, we're each here on our own soul journey through life. When our spirit enters a new body of a baby that spirit is ours and ours alone. We have to take responsibility for entering that tiny body, because it is the beginning of our journey. While we journey through life alone, we can share our journey with family, friends and partners along the way. However, we must always remember that this is our journey.

We alone are responsible for our fulfilment in life. We cannot expect anyone else to make us happy. Nor can we do it for anyone else. We can, however, share our happiness with someone else, just as they can share their happiness with us. If we put someone else's happiness first or hand the reins of our own life to someone else, then we are headed for disaster.

We are all likely to make this mistake at some time or another. There is a deep part of our collective subconscious which hooks us into this idea of allowing us to lean on others and of allowing them the responsibility for making us happy. But we need to be mindful at all times of not making this mistake.

To help you keep your thinking clear on this concept, try the following affirmation: *I take full responsibility for my own being and I am joyful in this.* Say it aloud to yourself every day, and picture in your mind's eye the colour pink, for this is the colour of love. When you love yourself enough, you will never allow yourself to slip into opting out of being responsible for your own wellbeing in life.

If you repeat this exercise daily you will be amazed at how much easier and happier your life will become because you are clearly stating to the universe your needs. You are choosing the future for yourself, not for your partner or anyone else. Do this exercise and be thrilled by the power of your own personal connection to the energy of the universe and experience a more joyful and rewarding life.

When we recognise who we are and understand that we all have the right to be treated with love and respect, we can easily recognise when we are not receiving these positive aspects from people around us, and speak up and get a better deal for ourselves.

Whether or not we have discovered who we really are, we need to remember always that we are very special and we deserve happiness in our life. That said, it is our spiritual duty while we are here on earth to do the absolute utmost that we possibly can to learn our own lessons and to grow wise in order to live a balanced, happy and fulfilling existence.

When we enter our physical bodies as souls, we automatically take on the commitment of honouring ourselves at the highest possible level by growing as much as we can. This then becomes a commitment to our highest selves to do the best we can for our souls to progress.

We all need to learn how to speak for ourselves. It is so easy to tell someone to speak up where we think they should. But it is another matter entirely to learn how to speak up ourselves. If you are in a situation in life where you need to say something, but lack the courage to do so, then maybe the following insights will help you:

First, recognise that you have rights. You do not have to subjugate yourself to someone else's needs—your needs are more important to you than someone else's needs. Of course, there are times when you do have to put your own needs on hold to attend to someone else's—but that should only be temporary and not an ongoing pattern in your life.

You also have strength—most of which you, like all of us, use only a minute amount of.

Speak up honestly and caringly. Say your piece, and never regret your move in doing so, no matter what the results. Remember, the more you speak up, the easier it is in the future to do so again. Practice makes perfect.

So often we become so dependent on our relationships that we allow ourselves to be dominated rather than risk the other person walking away. I first met Janine when she came to see me for her very first reading. She was a most unusual lady. She held a very high profile job and yet she appeared to be shy and withdrawn. Her life was so regimented that she seemed almost to be imprisoned by it. I was surprised that someone who appeared to be so closed to life and to the opportunities for enjoyment and for spirituality would bother to come to a psychic for advice.

In spite of the heaviness I saw around Janine, I liked her immediately. This heaviness appeared psychically as dark, dull greyish-black tones of colour in her aura. And yet buried beneath this I found a truly beautiful soul. I quickly realised that the way Janine presented herself to the world was an outward reaction to the inner struggle she was experiencing in her life.

In essence, she was a truly good person. Her high-powered job was vital to her wellbeing in that it prevented her from cracking both emotionally and mentally. It provided a necessary escape from her inner vulnerability. Without her position of power in her work I feared Janine would not cope at all with life. Her troubles seemed to centre around her marriage to a younger man, who was domineering not only with Janine but with their four boys. The boys were teenagers and they feared their father just as much as she did.

During the first part of the session Janine resisted my comments. Each time I stated that I could see her suffering she argued that her long marriage was quite fine and that she was doing well. She refused to discuss any negative aspects about her marriage and asked me to focus more on her career. This I did. I could find nothing but great success in Janine's future concerning her career. Towards the end of the session Janine asked me if I would just tell her whether I could see a move of house for the family. I told her, truthfully, what I saw. 'Your husband would never allow a move even though you and your sons would love to move.'

With this, Janine burst into tears. She sobbed and sobbed, telling me that this was true. Her husband was a tyrant and he was not ever going to put himself out for the family, no matter what. A breakthrough at last, I thought. The session continued. Janine admitted that her life was hell and that she hated her husband for his cruelty to which she had been subjected ever since they married twenty-eight years ago.

I felt truly upset as Janine went on to tell me the extent of her husband's cruelty both to herself and her sons. As she sobbed her way through these stories I could see that she both hated and feared her husband immensely. 'What would you really like to do with your life?' I asked her. Janine peered at me through her glasses and without hesitation she exclaimed, 'I would like to leave him and start a new life.'

'Well, could you afford to keep yourself?' At this question Janine smiled. 'Oh yes,' she said, 'I've been working all my life and I've saved money that David doesn't even know I have.' I was delighted. 'Then there's nothing to stop you from finding a flat for yourself and your sons if you want to,' I pointed out.

The simplicity of this truth hit Janine and she agreed. We went on to explore just how capable Janine was. I explained to her that she was entitled to a lot more control over her own life than David would permit, and that she had every right to happiness and not to be bullied for the rest of her life.

The session finished with a new woman sitting in front of me. She even looked different. Janine promised to telephone me in the future to tell me how she was going. I waved her goodbye with the promise that I looked forward to hearing from her soon.

Time passed and I heard nothing. I had often wondered how she was doing, then one morning some two years later, I answered the phone and was delighted to hear Janine's voice. She sounded so very happy. She told me that she had changed her life completely since we last met. She had moved into a lovely waterfront home that was everything she had dreamt of. Her boys were living with her. They were happy and her divorce had gone through some six months previously. She told me that she never had one moment of doubt about her decision to move on, and her husband had since retired from his job and had moved to another state. She was happy at work and pleased with her choice to make a better life for herself and her family.

When Janine came to visit me a few weeks later she had certainly changed. Everything about the way she looked made her appear younger—she had a lightness about her which was truly surprising. Janine and I became friends and I truly enjoyed seeing her enjoying her life. I knew that the choice she had made would release her to become the happy soul that was her inner core.

For years Janine had not been true to herself, because she was living her life supporting a man who treated her very poorly. She was allowing this situation to continue for a long time—so long, in fact, that she almost lost touch with her true inner self. If Janine had kept on living as she had been doing for much longer, I could see that she would have missed out on experiencing true happiness and contentment. This would have been terribly sad, for she certainly deserved to know what happiness is, as we all do.

No one else could do this for her—*she* had to do this for herself. I was so pleased to see how far she had progressed since our first meeting. Her courage to make changes in her life was rewarded by her happiness, her loving happy relationships with her sons, her enjoyment of her work, and her love and acceptance and respect for herself. So it was that the universe rewarded her for her courage and strength in taking steps to recognise her true self and changing her life to be true to that self.

Sometimes unhappiness comes from within us, rather than the situation around us. If we are not feeling fulfilled, it may be because we are not making the most of ourself, our gifts and talents, our work or our home. If we are not challenging ourself and growing spiritually, we will feel dissatisfaction with ourself and our life.

The way through unhappiness is to investigate the cause of the suffering. It won't help you to automatically assume it is the fault of someone else. In the contents of a marriage or partnership, discarding a partner for our own happiness is not a solution to our unhappiness. The universe will deal a severe blow to anyone who seeks to solve a problem in this way. We need to take responsibility for our own happiness, whether we are single or in a relationship, and when we do we will be rewarded over and over again.

Life is about loving and respecting ourselves as well as others. Often our closest relationships test us in this regard. If we lack self-worth, those around us will treat us accordingly. What we put out is what will come back to us. So, if we love and respect ourselves, we can expect love and respect in return.

Everyone has experiences that we call coincidences. However, I believe that there is no such thing as 'coincidence'. I believe there is a system operating at the psychic, spiritual level which is designed to keep people on the correct path through life. I believe there is a master plan, which I call universal justice, and that our spirit guides work to make things happen and in our lives these events appear as coincidence. But they are not; these events have been orchestrated and carefully planned by our angels. They may be 'destiny points' in some cases, but often they are not.

Humans have been given free will and we can choose what to do with our lives. However, if something is meant to happen, then it will, no matter what we do or how we try to prevent it. What we may think is coincidence may in fact be destiny.

This can happen when two people meet up after many years of being apart and they find themselves at the same place at the same time. Their paths to this meeting may be varied, simple or complex, but there is always a sound reason why the meeting occurred and the individuals involved will mutually gain some benefits from it.

Universal justice not only exists, but it operates at a very high level. Let me tell you how universal justice worked for Francine. The moment I met her I felt straight away that her psychic reading would be interesting, and it turned out I was right.

At the time, Francine was working as a carer for a government-backed agency. She had spent the last eighteen years in this line of work, and whenever an elderly, a handicapped or sick person needed her assistance, she would be available to do whatever was necessary to assist them. After devoting her time and energy to this task for so many years, Francine ended up with a back injury after lifting a patient. The pain and discomfort proved incapacitating and eventually her doctor told her that she would never again be able to do the work she was used to.

Francine was greatly disturbed by this as her job was her lifeline. She was devastated because she was a solo mum with two teenage daughters to raise. How could she pay her mortgage and provide the necessary comforts of life for herself and her daughters? she wondered. She decided to seek legal advice about her predicament, aware that if she were able to receive a pension, then perhaps the family could have enough to scrape by.

However, Francine soon learned that she was not entitled to a pension. Her legal advisor suggested that she attempt to sue the government department for compensation. This news quite upset Francine, but she could see that she had no other options. Having decided to take this step, she was next disappointed by the fact that her case would not be heard in the courts for another three years. Francine was now not only in severe pain, but was a mental and emotional wreck.

At the time of her first visit to me, she had waited the three years for her court case and she now had a date for the hearing which was just two weeks away. She wanted the guidance and strength to help her prepare for the outcome. As I tuned in I could see that universal justice was going to take over for Francine. I told her that she would win her court case and that the financial settlement she would receive would definitely allow her to have a safe and secure future. Tears sprang to her eyes as she processed what I was telling her. She thanked me at the end of the session and told me that she felt more positive and hopeful for the future. A few weeks later, Francine telephoned to tell me that she had won her law suit, and the settlement she received was enough for her to plan her life without the fear and despair which had plagued her for so long.

In Francine's case, universal justice stepped in to assist her to win her court case because basically she had not broken any universal laws. She was a good person, who had integrity and sincerity and who had generally been a kind, caring soul. She had always tried her hardest to do the right things in her life—and the accident that befell her forced her to utilise her strengths and not to give up her fight for a better life for herself and her two daughters.

Francine did not become a victim of her circumstances. When ill-fortune crossed her path she weighed up all of her options and she battled on. This courage, strength and determination that she displayed was seen by the universe as well worth rewarding, and universal justice stepped in to assist her with her battle with earthly justice and she rightfully won her lawsuit.

Universal justice will always be there when society's justice fails. In the story of Francine, society's justice failed to provide her with a pension to support herself and her daughters, but universal justice smiled upon her and provided her with the win in the law courts.

When we think back over our lives, we can each find incidents when universal justice has occurred, though we may not always know why. This happened to my client, Eleanor, to whom I gave a phone reading as she lived some distance away. During our session, Eleanor informed me that she had lost a charm from her charm-bracelet. Though the charm wasn't solid gold and therefore not particularly expensive, it was a gift and had great sentimental value to her. Eleanor wondered if I might be able to help her locate her missing charm.

I tuned in and saw the picture of a car and, more directly, the back seat of a car. I picked up that the car had been a recent purchase for Eleanor and that it wasn't a new car, which Eleanor confirmed. 'You have to lift the mat in the back of the car on the righthand side and you'll find what you are looking for,' I said.

A week or so later, Eleanor phoned and with great excitement she told me how she had looked under the mat in the car as advised, but instead of finding her charm she had found a ring. It was a solid gold band set with diamonds, and it didn't belong to her.

Though she was feeling somewhat disappointed that she did not find her missing charm, Eleanor was intrigued. Choosing the path of honesty, she immediately phoned the previous owner of the car, Pat, to inquire whether she had lost a ring. Pat said that she had in fact lost a ring, but was surprised to hear that Eleanor may well have found it in the car. The two ladies then agreed to meet so that Eleanor could return the ring. However, much to their surprise, the ring did not belong to Pat either.

With no other leads to follow, Eleanor took the ring to a jeweller to have it valued. She was overwhelmed to discover that the ring was extremely valuable and with it she could purchase her lost charm at least ten times over. Eleanor says she is now extremely grateful to have the ring and believes it was sent from her guides, whom she thanked for being so generous. It seems to me that there is no logical explanation as to why the ring was found in the car so perhaps this may have been an apport, a gift from the universe, which comes usually in the form of a small item and appears unexpectedly, and often without any explanation as to where it came from.

It is also an example of the universal truth: what you give comes back to you. Eleanor tried to find the owner of the ring out of honesty and kindness, and was rewarded by universal justice.

Sometimes, however, the opposite can occur when you lose an item, especially when you are certain it was safely in a particular place and that item just seems to disappear with no logical explanation. Chances are that your item has been removed by unseen forces. Often a spirit will do this if they wish to communicate something to you or they may simply wish to tell you that they are there.

There's also a good chance that the missing item will one day suddenly reappear. You may find it where you least expect it, with no logical reason. Don't worry if this happens to you. You are connecting with the spirit world, and all of its mystery and power.

Why them? I am often asked why is it that some people seem to have all the good luck and blessings in life, while others suffer and struggle with difficulty after difficulty? I believe that the answer lies once more in the universal truth of what you give is what you get back. However, even perfectly good and honest people may be challenged in life, because ultimately struggle is a part of our spiritual journey and we each have lessons to learn within our lifetimes.

Finding our way through life and relationships can be difficult or it can be easy and joyous. Much depends upon using the spiritual gifts of guidance from our higher selves as well as our angels. Along with these we should always take control or our lives and be prepared to change situations in our lives if need be. Being strong and courageous are useful traits to cultivate to help make our journey through life smoother.

To help you in times of trouble you might wish to follow this simple exercise and you will, with practice, find your higher self, and courage, strength and peace.

1. Lie down in a quiet place making sure you are very comfortable and that you will not be disturbed.

2. Close your eyes and listen to your inner voice. Your inner voice is underneath all the thoughts which run through your mind constantly. It will direct you to the right path. This inner voice is the same as your intuition, and intuition is a natural phenomenon which we are all given to help us through difficult times.

   Once you relax, letting go of all your conscious thoughts, you will find your inner voice. Do not question this inner voice, for it is giving you the correct guidance. This guidance may seem to be different from that of your conscious mind, and wherever there is a difference in the advice given, always follow your inner voice, your intuition.
3. When you hear this voice, heed its advice and take action. Your life will then begin to turn around and you will achieve progress in your journey.

Tell yourself over and over 'Every day in every way I am getting better and better. I am strong, I know my own mind, I am capable of knowing what the best situation is for myself—in fact, right now I can have what I want and I truly want——.' Tell yourself what you want, where you want changes made—tell yourself what these changes are.

Remember that keeping balance in our life and keeping every aspect of life in perspective is most important. Try to adopt an overview of your day-to-day existence. Remember that attitude plays a major role in how we deal with life. Learn to hear messages from your angels and recognise that all difficulties in life are only temporary. We are constantly growing and changing as we journey through life and the stronger we become the more rewarding the journey will be.

None of us knows the full shape and pattern of our lives. We can, however, be given glimpses that will propel us forward into a new awareness that can literally change our lives. We can only experience the adventure of life when we dare to be a little adventurous and follow our hearts.

Have a dream and use the power and strength of your mind to make it happen for you. You too will be surprised at the power behind your thoughts, which can manifest amazing things in your life.

A powerful demonstration of how affirmations work is seen in the results that can be obtained when using affirmations for healing. Many cancer patients know this is true. We can use our mind to envisage the cancer cells being bombarded by rays which destroy them. Results prove that this exercise helps in the healing for cancer patients. People with other illnesses can use this technique as well.

If you use affirmations on a daily basis you will see changes in your life. Positive affirmations carry a strong message to the mind, and healing and happiness can result. Turn your affirmations to any area of your life you wish to change. You can open yourself up at every level to create a better world for yourself. Repeat them often and results will ensue.

May the words of Mahatma Gandhi help to give us strength and understanding:

> 'If I have the belief that I can do it,
> I shall surely acquire the capacity to do it
> Even if I may not have it at the beginning.'

8

How angels can help us

If we are open to receiving information from the spirit world, we should also be open to acting upon that information. Too often we know what is right for us, what changes we should make to better our lives, and yet we remain bound on our earthly paths, virtually ignoring the messages from our guides.

It does take courage to let go of our lower consciousness and follow our intuition. But if we listen to our guides, the spirit realm and our higher selves, trust what we hear and then act on that knowledge, our lives will most certainly change for the better. We must also accept, however, that there are no guarantees in life that we will have an easy path. Some changes may not be to our liking. Sometimes, the change is extreme and we may feel shaken, lost and disoriented. But by following the spiritual guidance offered to us with courage, faith and trust, as well as taking responsibility for the decisions we make, the rewards of change will be countless.

We receive guidance from the spirit realm in many different ways. Our spirit guides and guardian angels are always with us and lovingly protect us. We can draw great comfort from this once we accept that they can and do interact with us. This is exactly what happened with a young lady called Mary.

Mary was a delightful fifteen-year-old. Sadly, from the time she was twelve, Mary had suffered from cancer. Her cancer was in the form of tumours, which first appeared on her arm and later all over her body. Mary was very inspiring and uplifting to be with and when her mother, Janelle, brought her to see me, it was Mary who was always positive and philosophical about the fact that soon she would be passing on to the spiritual realm. She promised her mother that when this happened she would let her know that she was with her in spirit form. Mary kept her promise.

Janelle visited me a few weeks after Mary had succumbed to her illness. Janelle was happy to inform me that Mary had demonstrated how well she had adapted to her new home as was turning on lights in the house at night and music was often mysteriously heard coming from the unconnected record player. On the day of her funeral, Mary had mischievously played tricks with the car by starting up the motor for a few seconds even though the key was not in the ignition.

Janelle was greatly comforted by these strange occurrences and was assured that her lovely daughter was safe and happy in the realm of spirits. Not all of us would be comfortable receiving such direct interaction from our spirit friends, but most people are delighted when an angel connects directly with them in a loving way. This was so for Helen.

Helen came to see me for a reading about her son, Paul, who had recently died. Helen was quite sad and upset at losing her much-loved son in an accident and was grieving so much that nothing could comfort her—nothing except Paul!

Paul was quite pleased that his mother had sought spiritual assistance to help her to deal with his passing. As we progressed with the session, Paul gave her many messages which showed her that he had accepted his death and was ready to progress with his new life as a spirit. At the end of the session he told her that soon she would meet a woman who would offer her a brown bracelet, and that this was really a present from him to his mum, whom he loved so much. He hoped that she would stop grieving so much and be comforted by the gift, which would remind her that he loved her and would always be with her in spirit. Helen found his message difficult to believe, but thanked me for the session and promised to tell me if she ever received the present.

Three weeks later an excited Helen phoned to tell me that a woman at the hospital which Paul had attended before his death had asked her if she would accept a present from her, as she felt sad for Helen in her grief. Helen took the gift and unwrapped it to find a lovely bracelet made of brown beads. Helen was elated and thrilled to receive the gift that her beloved son had promised he would give her. Helen now truly believed in angels.

Guides and angels are always with us. They send messages to us through books that we find, music that we hear and through people we meet. They will answer us if we ask for their help. If you are concerned about an issue and feel that all the answers have evaded you, then simply stop and ask your angels for answers. They do hear you. Stop worrying and continue to go about your daily routine, and suddenly you may be pleasantly surprised to just get the answer to your problem. Angels will give you the right answers. Try to accept the answers and things will work out for you.

You might wonder how we can meet our guardian angels. One way is through meditation. The exercise below can help you with this.

1. Sit or lie down comfortably—be relaxed and free from interruptions.

2. Close your eyes and allow yourself to focus on gently relaxing your body. Start with your head and work down to your toes. Tell yourself to relax all the muscles in the various sections of your body. Feel the tension draining away from your head, shoulders, stomach, back, buttocks, arms and legs. You may like to play some gentle music or you may prefer complete silence.
3. Once you have relaxed from head to toe, imagine yourself in your favourite place, like a lovely cool forest where the plants and trees are vibrant and colourful. Experience and feel the peace in the forest—the softness of the lush green grass, and smell the perfume of the wildflowers that carpet the ground.
4. As you relax and breathe in the atmosphere, become aware of a gentle and loving presence. An angel appears before you and you are overcome by the love you feel. You are feeling safe and secure and very much at peace.
5. As the images become clearer, listen to the words of your angels—what is she/he telling you? How do you feel? And what do you wish to say to her/him?
6. Enjoy this wonderful encounter and remember you can ask questions of your angel and receive answers to guide you.
7. When you are ready to say goodbye to your special angel, gradually allow yourself to come back to your waking state.

This exercise can be enjoyed as often as you like, and you will benefit from practising it.

Life can and will bring many good things our way, but we have to do our bit. If we are prepared to do our share, the spirit world will meet us halfway. This is a universal truth which applies to each and every one of us.

If you decide to step out in life and muster all your courage and have faith, then your angels will meet you and will help you along your way. Once you have made a decision to be brave and to take steps to change a situation in your life that is unbearable, then hold on to that decision. Be strong and recognise opportunities when they are given to you. Never settle for less that what is right for you, and while you continue to love yourself and show kindness to others, your angels will guide and protect you.

Of course we must have courage and faith if we are going to make massive changes in our lives. However, when we are going through difficult times, it's helpful to remember that a bad thing never lasts—life changes constantly and nothing remains exactly the same. This is a universal law, so we can look forward to the time when life will be better.

Jane's story is a good illustration of this point. Well groomed and seemingly confident, Jane was in her early forties. Before we started our session she told me that she was going through a very difficult phase in her life and that nothing seemed to be giving her any success or happiness.

As I began the reading, I discovered Jane had left a marriage in which her husband Jim had been unfaithful. This man seemed to be very selfish. Over the twenty years of their marriage, Jim had many affairs with other women which Jane knew of, but had managed to convince herself that she loved him anyway. She was always there for her husband and when his affairs turned sour Jane would even help pick up the pieces for him.

Finally, when Jane found out that Jim was having an affair with her best friend, whom Jane had trusted and confided in many times, she rallied enough courage to end the marriage. Jane took her young son William with her and found a comfortable apartment to call home, determined to make a better life for them both.

Over the next two years, Jane learned to cope on her own. During that time, she divorced Jim and, although she was only awarded a small settlement as Jim had always squandered their money, Jane was pleased to have that phase of her life over.

When I first saw Jane, however, she had lost her job. Worse still, the company she had been working for had not paid

Jane for a month. She certainly was not able to support herself and William without a job, and even though she had gone for many interviews she had not been able to secure another job.

Jane was basically an optimist, but her optimism had turned to pessimism as her situation became more dire. She was starting to wonder if she had made the right decision in leaving her husband. She wanted me to check psychically if she was still on the right path and if there was anything else that she could be doing to improve her life.

I tuned in and immediately Jane's guide appeared and said that soon the job she was desperate for would be given to her. She had to swallow her pride and ask her friend in another state for a personal loan to tide her over until the new job arrived. Jane was surprised, but confirmed that she had indeed been thinking about asking a friend for financial help.

Jane's guide also told her that she was being tested and she must find the courage to keep going. Jane was on the right path, despite the struggles she faced, but it was important that she did not lose her faith—that was her lesson to learn. Her guide then assured Jane that she had the strength to succeed.

At the end of the session, Jane told me she now believed that no matter how desperate she was feeling, she was still so much better off than she would have been if she had stayed with her unfaithful husband. Even though her situation seemed impossible, she knew that her courage was being tested and she must forge ahead.

And sure enough, a few weeks later Jane rang to tell me she'd found a great job. She had even been able to borrow enough money from her friend to pay the rent until her first pay came in. She was ecstatic that her courage and faith had finally been rewarded, and more so that they had been strengthened and renewed.

We can receive help in many ways from our guardian angels. A woman called Heather discovered this fact when she recently visited me for a reading.

We had settled in to the session when I realised that her father was in the room with us in spirit form. I told Heather about the elderly man. From my description she knew that this was in fact her dad. She was pleased that he had found contentment in his new home, having adjusted well to his passing some six months previously. Toby told Heather to stop worrying about what he had decreed in his will. Heather had received more than her brother in the will and she felt that perhaps her father did not really want this to be the case now. In fact, Toby reassured her that he wanted to reward Heather for her kindness to him during the final years of his life. She had always been there for him and had showed him great kindness and caring. He wanted the will to remain just as he had written it. No changes were required.

With this information firmly in her mind, Heather was able to accept that her dad's wishes would be followed without any of the guilt she had been feeling. She had definitely been helped by the spirit of her father.

When we do succeed in overcoming our problems, the spirit world is truly generous in rewarding us. If you think back over your life, I'm sure you will remember times when you were happy and everything fell easily into place for you. These times are rewards for the spiritual tests you have passed and the hurdles you have overcome.

For every action there is an equal and opposite reaction. This is not simply a law of physics, which you may have learned in school, it is also a law of the universe. This means if we do something good and positive, we will be rewarded with something good and positive in return. If we do something negative, we will experience something negative in return. If we are strong and try to overcome our problems, we will gain more strength and will succeed in life. If we are weak and do not try to overcome our problems, we will find life difficult and unrewarding. What we give is what we will get back.

So it is that the angels are always with us, sending messages and comfort and opportunities if only we are willing to listen and accept them. When we combine this truth with the power of our own mind, we can manifest great things in our lives.

Conclusion: Some thoughts to light your way

I have been asked many times about why I have been given the gifts of clairvoyance, clairaudience and mediumship. The answer lies in who I am at the soul level. As souls, we have many incarnations and we grow throughout these visits to the earth plane. I have been here many times, just as you have, and the knowledge I have collected enables me to have the privilege of facing a life experience (the loss of my daughter), which provided me with the catalyst necessary to open up my gifts. We all have our individual journey based upon many lifetimes and we each will find the right avenue to experience it.

From my own journey in this lifetime I have learned many things. The most important lesson for me is the fact that we are all connected at the soul level. We all are a part of each other. All living things are made of the same matter—water, minerals and chemicals—and these are also found in the landforms and environment, the earth.

But while every living thing is connected, we are each individual souls, and so are vastly different from each other. So while you and I are travelling to eternity together, we each have our own path to follow. The lessons we have to learn in this life are unique to us. We can learn from the lessons of others, but we have to pass our own tests.

As we progress towards enlightenment, we begin to understand that this earthly life operates in ways that are chosen, coordinated and planned. We begin to recognise that there is an unseen world of spirits, guides and masters who will assist us if we ask. Once we absorb and act upon this understanding, we will grow and change in our thinking, our behaviour and how we live our lives.

Sometimes, though, it takes a lot of courage to stay on our path towards enlightenment. We may have to sacrifice parts of life we do not wish to. Or we may find ourselves feeling lost and alone. During these times, we need to muster all of the courage, strength and faith that we have within us and see the bigger, higher picture of our lives. Remember that all things—good and bad—are in a state of constant change and it's up to each of us to make sure that this change is always for the better.

Life is a great leveller and no one person is better than anyone else. We are all equal in the eyes of the spirit world. Throughout many lifetimes we will ultimately all face the same spiritual tests, we all have the same weaknesses, and most importantly the same strength and tools to handle any challenges in our lives.

As we grow we begin to understand that this earthly life operates in ways that are set, coordinated and planned. We begin to recognise that there is an unseen world of spirits, guides and masters who will assist us if we ask. Once we absorb and act upon this understanding life takes on a new glow.

We need to honour and respect all life, for we are all equal and connected in spirit. By following our higher selves and our guides, we will learn that the best path to fulfilment is to live all our lives with love.

Your life is your journey from beginning to end. You chose it and you have all the tools to make it a wonderful adventure. More than this, you are unique, so be proud of yourself. Love, honour and nurture yourself. Recognise the magnificence and beauty of your own being.

Throughout your journey you will share your life with other people, and this should be enjoyed. However, do not compare who you are or what you have achieved with anyone else. We each have our own path and the fact that we continue to progress is all that matters.

How far we progress is measured by the lessons we have learned over many lifetimes, and by our own willingness to grow. Remember that we can choose to grow spiritually or not. We may choose to just coast along through one or more lifetimes, but ultimately we all must face the same tests.

Difficult situations in our lives help us to grow. Many people seem to thrive no matter how difficult their lives are. This is because these old souls have learned many lessons and acquired great wisdom through their past existences, and so they can find inner peace no matter how difficult their lives may prove—they know that true reality is beyond this earthly world. They know that it is the attitude with which we face our difficulties that counts, not our problems themselves.

We might take many lifetimes to complete our set of lessons successfully, but we will. And as we gain this knowledge, we will also gain understanding and ownership of spiritual gifts. These gifts include peace, patience, endurance, kindness, empathy, forgiveness, truth, knowledge, understanding, wisdom, loyalty and love, as well as gifts of psychic ability, healing and enlightenment.

It is not an easy task to achieve all of this in human form, we are certainly limited by our weaknesses and prejudices, but it is *our* task, and fortunately for us we have many helpers along the way.

We have our angels, who are our spirit guides, and we have our loving family members and friends who have passed on, but whose spirits remain around us. We also have access to wise people here on earth, our partners, family, mentors and friends, as well as teachers, whoever they may be, to help us along the way. Most importantly, we have ourselves, and our Supreme Being.

God does talk to you through spirit, and He sends His messengers to protect you and give you wisdom. So don't ever be afraid to ask for help and guidance by connecting with your higher consciousness, where all truth lies. Learn to trust and follow your higher self, your intuition, for it will never let you down.

So, dear reader, if you see yourself as the Supreme Being sees you, you will know that you are precious and deeply loved. You will take pride in yourself and your life, and you will use all of your spirit-given gifts to make this life of yours truly count for yourself, your soul, and others that you meet on your journey to eternity.

I'd like to leave you with some thoughts to light your way. Remember that you are guided, protected and watched over by your guardian angels and your spirit guides. The souls of many are with you, always. Find and hold the inner peace which this truth reveals. You are more loved that you can ever know.

1. You are never alone.

With the help of this book, I hope you will realise that you *always* have your spiritual guide with you. In fact, you usually have more than one guide with you. You are much loved, aided and protected by your spirit guides.

Apart from these wondrous beings, you have the love and protection of your Supreme Being with you. So you can surely see what I mean when I say *you are never alone*.

2. You are unique and precious.

There is only one of you, and only you have your soul. No one else is you. Even if you have an identical twin, then your twin has his or her own soul, and that makes them unique too.

You are rare because there is only one of you, which also makes you precious. Enjoy your uniqueness, and be proud to be the only one of you that will ever be.

3. You are stronger than you know.

Yes, you really are. And whenever you use your strength, it continues to grow. You are more powerful than any challenge you may face. You will never run out of strength; it continually replaces itself. You have unlimited strength within you.

4. You are equipped to handle all situations in life.

You are never put into a situation in life that you can't handle. We all come into this life equipped with everything we need to deal with any situation we encounter, and succeed. You have the spiritual tools to overcome all challenges—it's up to you to *use* them.

5. A bad thing never lasts.

Things are constantly changing. This is universal law. Nothing remains exactly the same. If you are suffering, then give yourself strength and courage by remembering that 'A bad thing never lasts'. It will have to change—as all things do. So you can always look forward to that time ahead when your life will change.

6. Healing is in your hands.

You do have control over your own health. You *can* overcome your health problems by using the power of your own mind and by taking an active role in your own healing.

7. Love the moment you have.

It is wise to truly love, enjoy and appreciate the moment that you have because it, like you, is unique. Once this moment has gone, it's gone forever, and you will never experience *exactly* that moment again.

If you love each moment, you will soon begin to love your life, as your life is made up entirely of moments.

8. Love people and let them experience life.

If you truly love someone, then you will love them enough to let them have the full experience of their *own* life. After all, it's their life, not yours. You have your own life.

Try not to be too controlling of your loved ones—be gently in the background, giving them love, protection and wisdom to carry them through.

If they make mistakes, and we all do, then lovingly help them to correct their mistakes and to move on—just as we must do in our own lives.

9. Know your gifts and share them.

We all have gifts. No one is born without gifts. The secret is to find your gifts and to utilise and expand them, and then selflessly share your gifts with others.

10. Be grateful for who you are and what you have.

Give thanks to the Supreme Being for YOU. You are special, there is just one of you, so be lovingly accepting of yourself. Also be grateful for what you have—whether this is great or small—as it has been given to you by the Higher Realms.

11. Recognise your teachers.

Be aware of those you learn from, for they come in many different guises. Be aware that someone might be your spiritual teacher even if that is not immediately apparent.

Your children may be your best teachers. Your friends or your enemies may be your best teachers. Your teachers may be hard to find, but once you have found them, you should honour and nurture them, for they will serve you well.

12. Respect your fellow travellers.

We are all united and travellers on the same journey. We are all headed to the same destination—eternity. One day, we will arrive. Your enemy and your friend are going with you. No one is better or worse than you—the journey to eternity is a great equaliser.

13. Honour your master.

Always honour those who lead you and teach you in this life and, above all, always honour your master guide and the *master* of your being, your higher self.

14. Honour your parents.

Your parents were chosen to be your parents, by you, by your guides and by the highest power. They were chosen because they, as your parents, could give you the lessons that your soul needed for its growth in this lifetime. So always give to them the love, respect and honour that they are worthy of.

15. Wisdom comes from within.

You will never find more truth anywhere than the truth you have within yourself. *You* hold all the answers for *you*. All truth and knowledge about you can be found by inner contemplation. Trust the answers that come from your higher self. Your intuition will *always* be right for you.

16. Honour our earth.

Earth is precious and, like each of us, it is unique. It is the arena in which you play your role in growing and learning. The earth gives you many wonderful gifts, including air, water, food, shelter and other souls. Without these you would not survive. We must all honour, nurture and protect the earth because it gives us life.

17. Life is to live.

Do not withdraw from life, for every moment is yours to live. Enjoy your life—experience it to the full—for you will never have *this* life again. Make your life a highlight of your soul's journey.

18. Take every opportunity to grow.

It takes courage to grow. It takes strength and fortitude to grow. The more you use your courage, strength and fortitude, the more of life you will experience.

Our spirit guides consistently offer us opportunities for growth. However, it is up to us to weigh up each opportunity before deciding whether or not to take advantage of it. Importantly, we should never take an opportunity to grow at the expense of ourselves or others—always think of the wellbeing of all concerned.

19. Nurture your inquisitive nature.

We have each been given a mind to use and we are all inquisitive. We all seek answers constantly. It is good to have questions, it is good to explore.

Sometimes, however, our inquisitiveness may lead us to trouble. So always consult and trust in your higher self—then you can't go wrong.

21. All things are possible.

If you have an idea, and it feels right for you and harms no one, then go for it. You can make your dreams come true. Don't hesitate to dream—anything in life is possible. Trust the highest power, your guides, yourself and your dream, and wait for the wonderful results.

22. Be open to change your beliefs.

Don't get stuck. People with closed minds often become stuck in life. All things are possible, so why not open up to the possibility of new concepts? You will be pleasantly surprised when you are open to new thoughts and ideas. Being open allows you to evolve and grow.

23. Miracles happen every day.

You witness so many miracles everyday that you forget how to recognise them. Open your eyes and see the miracles before you, you will be amazed by how many things appear.

You are a miracle. This world is a miracle. All the love that abounds is a miracle. Creation is a miracle and this is everywhere. So miracles happen everywhere, everyday.

24. Value your friends.

Never take your friends for granted. No matter how close you are to your friends, let them know often how much you value their friendship.

25. Surrender to the Supreme Being.

The Supreme Being loves you. When someone truly loves you, you are safe with them. True love means safety and security and total acceptance. The Supreme Being loves you absolutely and completely. His love is selfless and all-encompassing.

No living being could ever love you so utterly and completely—so why not love the universe and tell the Supreme Being that you love this world that is created by love. He will be with you *always*. There is no higher form of love.

Frequently asked questions

Question: When did you realise you had psychic gifts?
Answer: I did not know as a child that I had psychic abilitites, except for a couple of visions, like the Egyptian hieroglyphic eye which I used to see when I was about three years old. It was only after my baby daughter, Katherine, died that I became aware spiritually.

Question: How do you know that your predictions will prove to be accurate?
Answer: I don't. Only when a prediction happens do I know that I am accurate.

Question: How do you know things about people?

Answer: Information is given to me by spirit guides. When I am reading for a client, their spirit guides, who hold all knowledge about the client, tell me what they want the client to know.

Question: How do you get the information?

Answer: I see pictures (clairvoyance), and I hear words (clairaudience) and I feel things (clairsentinence). Sometimes I just 'know' psychically.

Question: How far ahead do you usually see things?

Answer: My readings usually span six to twelve months in advance, but this can vary. A psychic may see something that takes a long time to manifest. Time is difficult to predict because it is man-made.

Question: How can I connect with my spirit guide?

Answer: Meditate and visualise, and ask that your guides help you to communicate with them. You may seek help from a medium to connect you to the spiritual realm.

Question: Do we always have the same guides?

Answer: No, our guides change as our life situations change.

Question: Are the guides spirits of people we knew when they were alive?
Answer: Not necessarily. Some guides may be relatives or friends who have passed over, but this is not always the case.

Question: How many guides do we have?
Answer: This varies depending on our life situation. We all have a master guide who is with us throughout our entire existence, in all our earthy lives as well as on other planes.

Question: Why do guides come and go in our lives?
Answer: We draw guides to us for specific parts of our journey, depending on what lessons we need to learn and the guidance we require.

Question: What do guides look like?
Answer: They vary in physical appearance. Some are dressed in lavish costumes, some carry objects such as swords, scrolls or symbols which need to be interpreted. Most guides appear in human form but some appear just as pure white light. Some speak, some do not. Some do not appear at all but only speak or show their message. Some guides radiate pure energy, love or peace, while others can radiate very potent protective energy. Master guides may only appear as a face. All are amazing to encounter.

Question: Why can't we all 'see' and 'hear' psychically?
Answer: We all have the ability to utilise these gifts if we decide to do so in this lifetime.

Question: What are old souls?
Answer: Old souls have lived many lifetimes and are spiritually evolved.

Question: Do we have to reincarnate?
Answer: Yes, we do, until we are enlightened and until we are evolved to the point of perfection.

Question: Where do we go when we don't reincarnate any more?
Answer: We remain with the Supreme Being and exist in total peace and harmony with love, light and purity.

Question: How many lives do we have on earth?
Answer: As many lives as it takes to grow to enlightenment.

Question: Why don't I remember my past lives?
Answer: You do, but you can only access your soul memories if the knowledge will be useful in your current life.

Question: What happens when I die?
Answer: You will travel to another plane. Angels will assist you in your passing.

Question: Which plane will I go to?
Answer: That depends upon the level of your growth. You go where you will benefit the most for your journey.

Question: What are ghosts?
Answer: Ghosts are the blueprints of souls who have left the earthly realm.

Question: Why do ghosts appear sometimes?
Answer: Some are lost souls who have not yet moved on, while others appear in places they are comfortable with. Only a few, however, appear to be mischievous: There are negative spirits just as there are negative people.

Question: How do I banish a ghost?
Answer: If necessary, tell the ghost to go: Don't be frightened. You have more power than the ghost.

Question: How can I learn more about the spirit realm?
Answer: The best way is to read and associate with people who are spiritual.

Question: How can I be in tune with the spirit realm?
Answer: Be conscious at all times that messages are being relayed to you in many ways. Always trust your intuition.

Question: Can a psychic tell me the wrong thing?
Answer: Psychics can make mistakes. We can only relay the information to you as we see and hear it.

Question: Why didn't the psychic tell me about problems I would have along the way?
Answer: Again, we only relay the messages we receive. However, many psychics choose to see only the good things coming for a person.

Question: Do you see death in readings?
Answer: Not usually. Only if the person's guides wish it to be shown, which is rare, and even then it is only shown if it can be changed, such as a health warning.

Question: Do you always see auras around people?
Answer: Everyone has auras, but I usually have to 'tune in' to see them.

Question: Are you always tuned in?
Answer: No, I am in charge of my gift. I only use it when necessary, to help people.

Question: Can I lose my knowledge and level of awareness once they are attained?
Answer: No, once your spiritual knowledge is attained, nothing can undermine that. You will only continue to grow.